£3.50

CH00835798

SINGER, SONG AND SCHOLAR

edited by Ian Russell

 Sheffield Academic Press

Copyright © 1986 Sheffield Academic Press

Published by
Sheffield Academic Press
The University of Sheffield
343 Fulwood Road
Sheffield S10 3BP
England

Typeset by Sheffield Academic Press
and
Printed in Great Britain
by Dotesios Limited
Bradford-on-Avon, Wiltshire

British Library Cataloguing in Publication Data available

ISBN 1-85075-054 8

CONTENTS

SINGER, SONG AND SCHOLAR

Introduction

The papers in this volume represent the fruits of a series of conferences organised by the English Folk Dance and Song Society, on its own, and in conjunction with either the Centre for English Cultural Tradition and Language at the University of Sheffield or the Institute of Dialect and Folklife Studies at the University of Leeds, between 1982-1984. Whilst there is a wide divergence of approach and much variety in subject matter, they indicate the upsurge of interest in folksong research that has developed during the last two decades in the United Kingdom. What was formally an interest circumscribed by music and song is now informed by the various disciplines of social anthropology and ethnomusicology, social, economic and political history, cultural enthnography and media studies. The notion of folksong, isolated within a cultural vacuum, is one which can no longer be seriously entertained. The quest for new directions is a laudable one and an indication of the vitality of scholarship, but it is not in itself a panacea. The way ahead may prove to be as elusive and deceptive as a blind alley. It is with this figure of speech in mind that the first contributor, Georgina Boyes, warns against subjectivity on the part of fieldworkers and highlights their inability to recognise and identify the vernacular tradition around them. She feels that too often the concerns of the researcher lie only with acknowledged singers who are examined solely from a diachronic viewpoint.

In the three fieldwork studies that follow, each takes a contextual focus of contemporary tradition that avoids such blind alleys. Jim Carroll's account of the Irish traveller, Michael McCarthy, presents the vibrant culture of the social outcast whose strength of tradition seems inversely proportional to his relative status, on the margins of society. Arthur Howard, the Pennine sheepfarmer, was a very different singer, but he shared concerns common to all accomplished performers through his need to sing songs to suit the occasion. In my paper I have tried to show that this criterion of appropriateness manifested itself in a series of largely distinct repertoires. Carole Pegg's paper shares a rural focus and a concern with choice, but her perspective is much broader. She chooses to examine, not the individual component parts of musical tradition, but rather the genres of music preferred by the various communities in and around Blaxhall in East Suffolk, and how these preferences may relate to the structure of that society. The whole theoretical question of the relationship between song and society is explored by Michael Pickering, whose examination of social context and the reasons for the contextualisation of songs represents an important contribution to our understanding.

Within the generic term 'song', as used in the title to this volume, lie folksong, vernacular song, local song, popular song, and traditional song, all vying to provide the *mot juste*. Permeating such constructs is the concept of performance on one hand and, on the other, the artefact, the piece of paper on which a song is noted down. Alan Bruford explores how song manuscripts function in the context of Orkney and Shetland.

Whereas Michael Pickering has offered us an understanding of song within social context, Dave Harker has no intention here of providing us with a similar discussion from a historical point of view (for that the reader should refer to his article in *Folk Music Journal*, 5 (1985), 48-82—'The Original Bob Cranky?'). Rather the author outlines the dialectic chosen to achieve this end. He writes with enthusiasm of his 'history workshop' experiences and how through inter-action by an informed group they can enrich our appreciation and knowledge of how song and history interrelate.

It is hard to imagine that any new direction in folksong research could have been taken without the guiding hand of A.L. Lloyd and his brilliant *Folk Song in England* (1967). Our final set of three papers and a bibliography bear testimony to the importance of Bert Lloyd and his scholarship. In his tribute, Leslie Shepard describes the man he knew as a friend and contemporary, a writer of talent and a singer of presence. In his concluding insight—'a romantic at odds with a scholar'—Shepard points the way to our understanding of Bert Lloyd in the studies by Roy Palmer and by Vic Gammon. Just as we must credit Lloyd with the emergence of the serious study of industrial folk song in England, so we must also acknowledge the impetus he gave to the study of songs within an historical perspective. Lloyd may not always have been right in detail but he certainly had the essential vision of a major pioneer. Dave Arthur's bibliography hopefully illuminates the way to a comprehensive biography.

Singer, Song and Scholar could have been a book just about A.L. Lloyd—it would have fitted neatly. Instead, however, this volume provides the reader with an up-to-date sampler of the strength and variety of scholarship that occupies the field once held by Lloyd and his contemporaries. Whilst it is true that none of our current writers hold the same intellectual dominance, this is in no way a bad thing, for it indicates that each study represents an important differing aspect of research, worthy of further exploration in its own right. It is inconceivable that any one scholar might attempt at the present time the type of synthesis provided by A.L. Lloyd, so much new territory has since been discovered, and remains uncharted and unfamiliar.

IAN RUSSELL

NEW DIRECTIONS-OLD DESTINATIONS: A CONSIDERATION OF THE ROLE OF THE TRADITION-BEARER IN FOLKSONG RESEARCH*

Georgina Boyes

The nature of the information English researchers in folksong feel desirable and necessary for a full understanding of their subject has undergone considerable change since major collecting began in the nineteenth century. In this paper, I would like to examine some of the ways in which this altered focus of research has affected folkloristic perceptions of the role of the informant. By doing this, I hope to assess the new concepts of tradition developing in English folkloristics in terms of their relevance to informal creation, performance, and transmission of songs in contemporary culture.

The ideology underlying the efforts of the early Folksong Revival collectors is well known. Like the early folklorists,[1] they saw themselves as the recorders of a dying form of culture. Folk music, in common with other traditions, was felt to be under threat from modern life—where both high and popular culture ignored its aesthetic and historical value.

The source of the expressive culture which folksong collectors wished to see more fully appreciated, however, did have certain problematic implications. It comprehended modal music with impressive historical and cultural associations and had notable academic and artistic possibilities. It existed, however, almost entirely in the performance of the semi-literate working class. This apparent paradox was explained in terms which both reinforced the status of the music whilst distancing it from its performers. It was proposed that generally, traditional art forms, especially narrative and music, did not originate with the 'folk', but in fact derived from a *gesunkenes Kulturgut* of materials created by

*This paper was given at the 'Traditional Song' conference at Leeds, 20 November 1982. An earlier version was published in *Folksong Research*, 3, no. 4 (March 1985), 51-56.

the upper classes. These aesthetically superior creations had then, over time, been passed on to or adopted by the lower class folk.[2]

The view that the folk 'are unable to create anything equal to the songs which they have received'[3] was widely voiced and accepted. Moreover, its corollary, that traditions can only degenerate over time, is still implicit in some folkloristic writing today.[4] This devolutionary premiss was so prevalent in folksong studies that the term *zersingen* (literally 'singing to pieces') was developed to describe the process of degeneration songs 'suffered' as a result of performance by the folk over the years.

It would be simplistic to suggest, however, that this separation of performers from their material was a cynically conscious process within the ideology of all the early collectors. In terms of their attitude to informants, for example, some fieldworkers set a standard above the liberals of their time. Even today, few would quarrel with Sir Lawrence and Lady Gomme's 1916 suggestion that prospective folklorists would find 'the work of collection will be a delight and pleasure. . . for it will introduce them to men and women of great chracter and individuality'.[5] More strikingly still, it has taken almost eighty years for Sydney Addy's fieldwork practice of always requesting permission of the informant before recording, including in his articles biographical details of the people he interviewed, and giving them copies of the papers when published, to become widely adopted.[6]

These standards were not, however, universal. Throughout the period in which the study of traditions was becoming institutionalised, writings were produced which simultaneously proclaimed the high artistic status of the 'lore' whilst patronising, trivialising, and mis-representing the 'folk' from whom it was collected.[7] Although this should be viewed within the norms of the period, it is unfortunate that for a considerable time the majority of English fieldworkers at worst consciously exploited, and at best condescendingly romanticised their informants. Whatever the attitudes of individuals, however, it is clear that theoretical structures which effectively denied performers an active, creative role in traditional processes were implicit in folkloristic scholarship in England until comparatively recently. The resultant view of folksong has therefore, a number of serious limitations.

Historically, all informants, whether they merely knew a few folksongs, sang only for their own recreation in private, or were well recognised public performers with extensive repertoires, were identically regarded. Until pre-literate, traditional society had been 'devastated' by industrialisation, education and mass culture, it was accepted that every member of the folk had been a tradition bearer. The elderly women and men from whom Cecil Sharp and the Folksong Revivalists collected their material were therefore presented as remaining representatives of this era. Axiomatically few in number and now distinct from the rest of the population, there was little about them as individuals that was considered suitable for study. What was repeatedly stressed by middle class collectors was the long history and 'uncontaminated preservation' of the songs and their music over time.[8]

Today, however, the focus of folksong research has shifted from the item of tradition to performers and their performance. A song's text, history, and music is now seen as only supporting information within the fuller study of the context of a singer and her or his performance. To reach a complete understanding of the songs we collect, it is considered not only desirable, but necessary that a full life history, listing of repertoire, and detailed description of the social, psychological, and physical context of the tradition should also be recorded.[9]

It is generally accepted that a requirement of fuller contextual information represents a valuable change in the direction of scholarship which will provide a rounded picture of tradition. In principle, this proposal has much to recommend it. Empirical research on individuals and their relationship with specific types of expressive culture can only increase our understanding of the processes involved in artistic creation. The practical application of the new focus of research, however, has not been entirely cogent. In a number of areas, particularly those relating to the role of the informant as tradition bearer, concepts and strategies exist which set arbitrary and illogical limits on folkloristic examination of the processes and forms of performance.

The term 'tradition bearer' occupies a cardinal position in any examination of the development of folkloristic theory from the later nineteenth century to the present time. It would represent as acceptable a summing-up of the performer's role in the process of transmission to Cecil Sharp as it does for most researchers in England today. Indeed, the continued application of this concept when other aspects of nineteenth century theory have been put into question must in itself be seen as significant. If the concept of the tradition bearer is examined in the light of the change in folkloristic paradigms, several questions become apparent. The foremost of these are related to tradition itself.

Is 'tradition' item-centred and concerned with the handing-on of texts and tunes over time (*pace* Sharp)? Or has it developed a new application centring on the performer and the processes of informal perform-ance?[10] The answers to these questions can be examined in terms of two inter-related aspects of the concept of the tradition bearer's role:

1.   What is the nature of the tradition borne by tradition bearers?
2.   What role do tradition bearers play in performance/ transmission processes?

Until performance-centred definitions of folksong were developed, most folksong collectors in England had become increasingly clear about what they wanted to record—a specific range of songs which were the product of oral transmission over time—preferably those with no attributable authorship. This category is, as I have indicated elsewhere,[11] an arbitrary and artificial grouping which was not fully defined until the early twentieth century. Its reinforcement through specialist publica-tions and the work of collecting societies,[12] however, led to a comparatively unquestioned acceptance of its value for some consider-able time in England.

It is now widely agreed that some earlier views of folksong are too narrow. Francis James Child, the American ballad scholar, writing in the mid-nineteenth century felt that any version of a song traceable to a broadsheet was inevitably inferior. At this time, broadsheets and songbooks were widely produced. Cecil Sharp, working in England some fifty years later, continued to stress the supremacy of oral tradition over print, but did not find it unacceptable to 'fill out' an 'incomplete' text with broadsheet verses. He did, however, produce numerous lengthy condemnations of the popular mass culture prevalent in his own time, particularly music-hall songs and parlour ballads. In keeping with this folkloristic practice of tacitly accepting the mass culture of a previous generation as the folksong of today, contemporary fieldworkers will now generally record a tradition bearer's version of a music-hall piece without demur. Thus, in item-centred terms, there has been a comparatively broader approach to the songs of a tradition bearer.

It is, however, suggested that context and process, rather than item, are the new dimensions which are explored in the fresh direction folksong studies have taken. If this is so, current approaches to repertoire highlight a number of anomalies in its application. In his otherwise cogent and valuable study of John Maguire, for instance, Robin Morton provides a catalogue of what he terms the singer's 'full repertoire'.[13] If this listing is really to be taken as Mr Maguire's entire repertoire, it must be assumed that although apparently a Catholic, he didn't know so much as a fragment of a hymn or carol. Similarly, mass culture was all around him, but he'd never even hummed a half-chorus of 'White Christmas' or any other popular song whilst going about his work.

If the aim of the context-centred approach is to provide a fuller understanding of the interaction between performer and song, then all songs learnt and/or performed informally should be researched. In arbitrarily dividing active and passive repertoire into traditional and popular categories there is a considerable danger that songs of significance to performers will be ignored because of their theoretical unsuitability. In terms of definition, moreover, there seems little justification for omitting any song known to a tradition bearer from a repertoire listing when performer, performance, and context are the focus of research.

An examination of the second aspect of the tradition of tradition bearers presents a rather more complex, but interesting picture. Classically, the performance/transmission process in which singers were held to have learnt and re-produced their repertoire was entirely oral.[14] As has already been established, however, popular printed sources such as broadsheets were later accepted as playing a part in transmission—though the stress laid on oral tradition meant that the interaction was rarely discussed in any detail. Even more recently, songs learnt from sheet music, radio, and records have come to be recognised as forming a part of a performer's repertoire which shoud be noted. Though various media and forms of transmission are now considered an acceptable source of material, popular songs transmitted via the mass media are rarely examined in the same way as traditional songs. That such material is in fact a significant component of overall repertoire is rarely, but easily demonstrated. Alice Kane and Edith Fowke's *Songs and Sayings of an Ulster Childhood*, for example, convincingly shows the personal variation and integral unity of popular items within a performer's active and passive knowledge.[15]

Perhaps the major lacuna in current forms of examination of the role of tradition bearers in transmission/performance, however, is in the choice of subject for research. It seems that whatever position is adopted theoretically, in practice, individuals are only singled out for research when they are known to perform some traditional songs. A singer, therefore, has to be an old style tradition bearer for the popular songs in their repertoire to be considered for study.

An increase in information about and examination of the creativity of individual performers has been the most valuable aspect of the present application of the context-centred approach. Deepening knowledge of the interaction between life-history, personal aesthetics, choice of songs and the manner of their performance have added new dimensions to our understanding of the inter-relationship between individuals and transmission processes. By researching the workings of transmission only as it occurs in the specialist group we term tradition bearers, however, we set arbitrary and potentially misleading limits on our findings. If any individual takes the trouble to learn and informally perform any song or even finds a particular song aesthetically pleasing over a period of time, whether they are a tradition bearer or not, their reasons are important for an understanding of performance overall. They should, therefore, be studied.

The logic of a broader approach to context becomes still more apparent when specific categories of song are highlighted. The paucity of recorded examples of English lullabies, for instance, has led writers to suggest that the genre is rare in this country. Fieldwork, however, rapidly establishes the fact that English babies are frequently sung to sleep, but that the songs used are outside the accepted item-centred area of definition. In general, the songs functioning as lullabies in English tradition are 'popular'.[16] For at least the past sixty years, the traditional activity of lulling babies has been accompanied by any comparatively current song with a gentle but regular rhythm. Specifically composed lullabies (such as Brahms') and songs with textual references to night and sleep appear to be widespread initial choices. However, rhythmic songs of any kind favoured by the singer seem to be used subsequently, especially if the activity is performed over a long period. In spite, therefore, of a traditional function, and informal context of performance, the absence of a 'traditional' item again negates the role of a performer as a tradition bearer. Further, because there is no acceptable item, there has been no attempt to study this widespread form of traditional performance.

A still greater area of performance and creativity is, however, almost entirely undocumented by English researchers. Notable events still give rise to local ballads and parodies in profusion. Though few collectors today would entirely agree with Maud Karpeles judgement on locally composed Newfoundland ballads—that a singer 'certainly knew lots of songs but none she [Maud Karpeles] wished to hear',[17] new compositions are researched mainly when an accepted traditional singer like Belle Stewart has written them. Similarly, the body of material deriving from events like strikes has not produced English studies comparable in scope to Peter Narvaez's work on the Buchans miners' struggle with ASARCO in Canada.[18] For as long as tradition continues to be defined in terms of items, the creativity of performers will have a detrimentally uncertain status.

In personal terms also, there is still a need for re-appraisal of the relationship between collectors and the individuals they work with. While tradition bearers are defined by criteria which separates them from the rest of the community—by age, class, or education—there is a danger that equality of consideration will be lessened. The presentation of tradition bearers as a specialist group who are few in number gives association with them a status that can lead to statements such as:

> We should like to thank all those who guided us to the 'storehouses' [traditional singers]. . . . We hope they will be rewarded by seeing the names of *their own particular singers*, my italics . . . and by hearing younger folksingers quoting their names with reverence.[19]

Or, as in the School of Scottish Studies' notice at the 1979 International Society for Folk Narrative Research meeting to which bearers of various traditional narratives had been transported for the evening—

> Folk tales will be told on demand.

If the definition of tradition bearer operating in contemporary English folksong research practice is examined, therefore, it appears that the criteria used are relatively unchanged and their application is unjustifiably arbitrary. Tradition is all around us. Almost every individual knows songs they have either learnt orally or perform informally, but the number of people and contexts studied, written about, and recorded by folksong researchers is remarkably small. The increasing volume of publications dealing with historical sources also tends to support the view that researchers see little in their environment today that they consider traditional enough to engage their attention. The present form of contextual research developed in a relatively unstructured manner.

Within it, it seems that the concept of tradition applied by researchers is still circumscribed by the idea of the traditional item. Having established tradition bearers as being those individuals who know a body of items classified as traditional, most fieldworkers then take a circular path to the point that defines as suitable for traditional song research those items which are known by the individuals they classify as tradition bearers. Nowhere is there an attempt to examine aspects of informal performance except in cases where it approaches this self-fulfilling stance. For as long as the new direction taken by folksong research follows this route, it will continue to return to its old destination.

NOTES

1. See Georgina Smith, 'Literary Sources and Folklore Studies in the Nineteenth Century: A Re-assessment of Armchair Scholarship', *Lore and Language*, 2, no. 9 (1978), 26-39 for extended discussion of this topic.

2. This term was coined by Hans Naumann (*Grundzüge der deutschen Volkskunde* [Leipzig: 1922]) but had been current as a concept since at least the mid-nineteenth century. See A.L. Lloyd, *Folk Song in England* (London: Panther Books, 1969), pp. 55-58 for a comprehensive critique of this view.

3. J.R. Moore, 'The Influence of Transmission on the English Ballads', *Modern Language Review*, 2 (October 1916), 389.

4. Alan Dundes, 'The Devolutionary Premise in Folklore Theory', *Journal of the Folklore Institute*, 6 (1969), 5-19.

5. Sir Lawrence and Lady Gomme, *British Folk-Lore, Folk Songs, and Singing Games*, National Home Reading Union Pamphlets Literature Series, No. 4 (London: National Home Reading Union, n.d. [1916]), p. 3.

6. Sydney Oldall Addy (1848-1933) was probably the best fieldworker England has ever produced. See Smith 1978 for the reasons for his eventual disillusion and break with folkloristic research.

7. See *The Handbook of Folklore*, edited by Charlotte Sophia Burne (London: Folk-Lore Society, 1914) for an example of the disturbing combination of surface liberalism (pp. 3-4) and overt racism (pp. 1-19 *passim*) which underlay much of the theoretical writing of this period. This and other problematic aspects of contemporary folkloristics are discussed in David Harker, 'Cecil Sharp in Somerset: Some Conclusions', *Folk Music Journal*, 2 (1972), 220-240.

8. See my 'Performance and Context: A Study of the Repertoire and Performance Styles of a Folk Revival Singer', in *The Ballad Today: Proceedings of the Thirteenth Meeting of the Ballad Commission* (Addiscombe, Surrey:

January Books, 1986), for more detail of this development in folkloristic theory.

9. Current folkloristic views on this subject are presented in Mary Ellen Brown and Paul S. Smith, *Ballad and Folksong*, Cectal Research Guide No.3 (Sheffield: Centre for English Cultural Tradition and Language, 1982).

10. The context of performance for any item or process can be seen as a continuum ranging from the highly structured and institutionalised formal performance context such as a Coronation, Symphony Concert, or Civic Banquet to the informal *ad hoc* context of a joke telling session at a pub or singing in the bath. Placing a context in the continuum would depend on factors such as degree of institutionalisation, structuring of the event, forms of reward for performance, audience's and performer's expectations, and the number of times an event may be repeated.

11. Boyes, 'Context and Performance'.

12. See Smith 1978, for a more extensive discussion of this.

13. Robin Morton, *'Come Day, Go Day, God Send Sunday': The Songs and Life Story, Told in his Own Words, of John Maguire, Traditional Singer and Farmer from County Fermanagh* (London: Routledge and Kegan Paul, 1973), p. xii.

14. As for example, 'Nothing can properly be called folksong that has not been submitted to the moulding processes of oral transmission', G.H. Gerould, *The Ballad of Tradition* (Oxford: Oxford University Press, 1927), p. 3.

15. Alice Kane, *Songs and Sayings of an Ulster Childhood*, edited by Edith Fowke (Dublin: Wolfhound Press, 1983).

16. I am most grateful to BBC Radio Sheffield, Dorothy Shepherd and Nigel Hallam for their assistance with part of the survey on which these findings are based.

17. A fuller discussion of Maud Karpeles' fieldwork in Newfoundland is contained in Carole Henderson Carpenter, 'Forty Years Later: Maud Karpeles in Newfoundland', *Folklore Studies in Honour of Herbert Halpert: A Festschrift*, edited by Kenneth S. Goldstein and Neil V. Rosenberg (St John's: Memorial University of Newfoundland, 1980), pp. 111-124.

18. See *Come Hell or High Water: Songs of the Buchans Miners* (12-inch L.P. 1001, Breakwater Recording, 1977).

19. *Folk Songs of Britain and Ireland*, edited by Peter Kennedy (London: Cassell, 1975), p. viii.

'Mikeen' McCarthy   *Photo by Pat Mackenzie*

MICHAEL McCARTHY, SINGER AND BALLAD SELLER*

Jim Carroll

In 1973, Pat Mackenzie, Denis Turner and I made contact with several of the large number of Irish travellers that were to be found in and around the Greater London area. We started recording singers, having very little experience in this field and, in six weeks, had collected over a hundred songs and completed a list of potential informants that would keep us occupied for the next five years, if they were all to be followed up.

It became obvious to us that there was much more to be collected than songs and that we would have to evolve a method of work that would allow us to use the time we had available to the best advantage. Coincidentally, about the time we were reaching this conclusion, the London Borough Councils were putting into motion policies designed to clear their areas of travellers. Almost overnight, it seemed, all the people we were in contact with had been evicted from their sites and scattered all around the outskirts of London, making it virtually impossible for us to continue our work with them.

We decided that the best way to proceed was to index the collection, take a look at the material and see if we could not arrive at a method of work; it was nearly eighteen months before we took it up again. We had reached the conclusion that the best method for us was to concentrate our attention on a small number of informants and record not only songs but as much information on travelling life and culture as possible. We were able to meet up once more with our original contacts and begin

*This paper was given at the 'Traditional Song' conference at Leeds, 20 November 1982, and accompanied by tape-recorded examples. Transcriptions of Examples 1 and 2 have previously been published elsewhere, in 'Michael McCarthy: Irish Travelling Man', *English Dance and Song*, 45, no. 1 (1983), 11-14, and Example 3 in Sharon Gmelch and Pat Langan, *Tinkers and Travellers* (Dublin: O'Brien, 1975), p. 139. The transcriptions here are by Ian Russell.

work again, but progress was slow as most of them were camped a fair distance outside London and, as we were only able to work at weekends or evenings, the time we could spend with them was very limited.

One evening, after a long period of doing very little recording, we were drinking in a pub to the west of London when one of the travellers pointed out a man engaged (we thought) in conversation with several other men. We approached the group and found that in fact he was singing to them. We introduced ourselves and asked if he would be prepared to sing for us. He agreed and the following evening we began working with Mikeen McCarthy, work we have not yet completed after eight years.

Mikeen (Little Michael) McCarthy was born fifty years ago in Cahirciveen, a small town on the Inveragh Peninsula in County Kerry in the south west of Ireland. His parents followed the traditional travelling trades: tin-smithing, horse dealing, hawking, chimney sweeping and, like a number of travelling families, spent eight months of the year on the road and rented a house for the winter, thus enabling Mikeen and his four sisters to get a little education. In addition to these trades, Michael McCarthy, senior, spent some time abroad as a soldier in the First World War and as a miner and bare-fist prizefighter in South Wales. Both of Mikeen's parents were singers, his father being in great demand as one, among travellers and in the settled community in Kerry. His mother was an Ullagoner, one of the women who were called on to keen or lament at funerals.

Mikeen took up tin-smithing as his first trade but later became skilled as a caravan builder. Some of the beautiful barrel-topped vans that are now used to haul holidaymakers around the roads in the south west of Ireland were built by him.

During his youth, he worked with his mother at the fairs and markets selling 'the ballads', the song sheets that were still being sold in rural Ireland right into the fifties. These sheets, measuring about 12 inches by 5 inches, were printed on coloured paper and contained the words of one song. The trade was carried on almost exclusively by travellers. The songs appearing on the sheets were by no means all traditional. Titles mentioned to us were 'Little Grey Home in the West', 'Smiling Through', 'Home Sweet Home', and 'No Place Like Home', as well as 'Rocks of Bawn', 'Sailor's Life', 'Betsy of Ballentown Brae', and 'Willie Reilly and his Colleen Bawn'.

Mikeen was able to describe to us in great detail how these ballads were printed and distributed. Although, as I have mentioned, he had received some education, his writing ability was somewhat limited; his mother is still unable to read and write. They would go into a town or village where a market was to take place and approach a local printer. The words of a selected song would be recited to the printer who would take them down and an order would be placed for the required number. In Kerry, where the McCarthys traded, the sheets were illustrated with a picture that related to the song: 'A man's song would have the picture of a man at the top, a woman's would have a woman's head'. This does not appear to have been the case throughout Ireland; in County Clare we have been told that the sheets contained the words only, with no illustration.

When they were printed they were taken around the fairs, usually to the bars, and sold at a penny each, though sometimes, towards the end of the day, they would be sold for less. A seller had to be able to supply tunes for the songs on sale; quite often a transaction depended on this. Mikeen described how, at a fair in Tralee, a customer was so anxious to learn a song that he pushed a pound note into Mikeen's top pocket every time he sang the song through: 'I went home with eleven pounds that time'.

Attitudes to ballad selling appeared to have differed among travellers. Athough it was carried out almost exclusively by them, by many it was regarded as no better than begging: 'They thought it was a low trade, but I didn't, I was glad to do it. I still would if I had the chance.' Even Mikeen's parents disagreed about it: 'My mother thought it was okay, but my father didn't like the idea of his songs going on them; if he found out there'd be trouble.'

The songs that were selected for the sheets would depend on where they were to be sold: 'Some would sell well in one place and some in another. . . If you could get a song that nobody knew in that place, you had a winner.' Quite often Mikeen would be asked if he had any of his father's songs for sale. Such a request would be complied with the next time that place was visited.

The practice of ballad selling appears to have died out some time in the late fifties. One of the last songs to have appeared on a ballad was 'The Pub with No Beer'. These ballad sheets, along with the song page in the weekly magazine, *Ireland's Own*, have exerted a very strong influence, for good or ill, on the singing tradition in Ireland over the last fifty years. We have yet to meet an Irish traditional singer who has not learned songs from them.

We were interested to find that a song, entered in the Stationers'
Register in 1675, was still being sold on a ballad sheet right into the
1950s. Moreover, it is still popular among Irish travellers today as in
Example 1, which was recorded in late 1975.

Example 1

THE BLIND BEGGAR (Laws N27)

Michael McCarthy
Late 1975

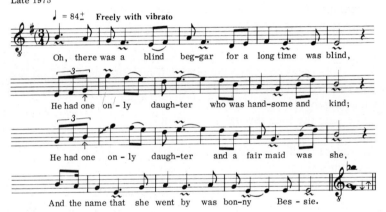

Oh, there was a blind beggar, for a long time was blind,
He had one only daughter who was handsome and kind;
He had one only daughter, a fair maid was she,
And the name that she went by was bonny Bessie.

The first came to court her was a rich squire so grand,
He courted lovely Bessie then all the night long,
Saying, 'My land, gold and silver, I will give to thee,
If you'll tell me your father, my bonny Bessie.'

Oh, the next came to court her was a captain from sea,
He courted lovely Bessie in then every degree,
Saying, 'My ship, gold and silver, I will give to thee,
If you'll tell me your father, my bonny Bessie.'

Oh, the next came to court her was a merchant so grand,
He courted lovely Bessie then all the night long,
Saying, 'I'll buy you some fine satins right down to your toes,
If you'll tell me your father, my bonny Bessie.'

Oh, my father he's a blind man that is very well known,
He is led by a dog and a chain and a bell,
He is led by a dog and a chain and a bell.
Will you roll into my arms, my bonnie Bessie.

Oh I'll buy you fine satins right down to your toes,
I'll build you a mansion right up to the moon,
. . .
And the blind man he laid down ten times as much more.

As well as information about the ballad sheets, Mikeen has provided us with many insights into the singing tradition in Ireland, especially concerning the singer's approach and relationship to his material. We had been working with him for over a year and had got to know him quite well when we decided to question him about how he felt about his songs; which songs he felt important, which songs he had learned just to sell, which ones he had picked up because he happened to be around when they were being sung. We got him to sing one of his songs, 'Betsy of Ballentown Brae' (Laws P28), and we asked him what he thought about while he was singing it. He furnished us with a complete description of all the characters in the song, what they looked like, what they wore, where they lived (not Ballentown Brae), and a description of the area where the action of the song takes place. None of this information is given in the text. He described the mental process that took place while singing as; 'like watching a film at the pictures, or watching television'. We asked him if this was the case with all his songs, to which he replied that he thought it was. We then took one of his non-traditional songs, 'I Wish All my Children were Babies Again', and repeated the procedure; he was unable to supply us with any information about the song. Then we asked him to sing 'Early in the Month of Spring' (Laws K12), to which he provided a full visual description, as with the first song. Again we took a non-traditional song, 'The Night you Gave Me Back my Ring', and once more he was unable to provide us with any description. We have found this visual identification with traditional songs common to most, though not all, of the singers we have questioned so far.

It has been our experience that, while all the singers we have recorded have no compunction in singing non-traditional material, country-and-western, parlour ballads, pop songs, etc., they do separate these in their minds from traditional songs, often having a term that describes the type of song (this is the case with both travellers and settled singers). One travelling woman we have been recording for some time now has given us over sixty songs and, though we are aware that she could easily double this number with non-traditional material, she has constantly avoided doing so: 'You don't want them, they're modern songs'. She told us that she doesn't like the 'modern songs', but is expected to sing them by other travellers, especially when she sings in the pubs. She describes all the traditional songs she has given us so far as her father's songs, even though, on questioning, she can remember exactly where she got all her songs, and it turns out that only half-a-dozen actually came from her father. So far, after nearly ten years work with Irish travellers, we have recorded less than a dozen non-traditional songs, although this has not been a deliberate policy on our part.

This differentiation also covers the way that the songs are sung. On one occasion when we were introduced to the brother of one of our informants, we were taken aside by another singer who told us that we shouldn't 'waste our time' with him as, even though he had the old songs, 'he can't sing them properly'. It turned out that the person in question was accustomed to singing country-and-western songs and everything he sang, including versions of 'The Outlandish Knight' and 'The Lover's Ghost', was given country-and-western treatment!

Mikeen McCarthy values his songs as belonging to a time that is now gone, along with the old trades and a way of life that, though by no means easier, was far more tolerable than today. Some of this attitude may be accounted for by the fact that one tends to look back on the past through the rose-tinted spectacles of hindsight, but there can be no doubt that all the travellers we have met got more satisfaction out of tin-smithing, caravan building, and horse trading than they do from today's main occupations of collecting scrap and shifting rubbish. Mikeen places the action of most of the songs we have questioned him about in locations he has visited during what he considers as 'better times'.

As a singer, Mikeen is by no means the most skilful we have recorded, but in many ways he is the most easy to listen to. His delivery can best be described as conversational and his approach narrative. The phrase used in the west of Ireland, to 'tell a song', sums up perfectly Mikeen's singing. In a folk club (he has appeared at the London Singers' Club several times), he will select a member of the audience to use as a focal point and sing to them. Whilst he is singing, he becomes totally engrossed in the story of the song.

As well as having a repertoire of fifty odd songs, he also has a large number of stories, ranging from the traditional tales and legends of Ireland, to stories and anecdotes about travelling life. This aspect of his culture is still very active and he is constantly coming up with fresh material that he has recently learned. Two months ago he told us a version of 'The Bishop of Canterbury' tale that he had heard that week. On one occasion he told us a joke he had just heard from another traveller, about a travelling couple with a large family, in conversation with a wealthy landowner with no children. This he told us as a dirty joke, in the third person, with just basic narrative and containing no detail. A couple of weeks later he re-told us the joke, which had by then undergone a number of changes and additions. About a month later he told us it again but, by then, it had been padded out with much more description and completely personalised, that is, told as having happened to him and his wife. He has a number of stories in his repertoire which are tale versions of traditional songs, including 'the one about the rich girl who ran off with a gypsy'. Example 2 is a tale that shares its plot with the ballad, 'Get Up and Bar the Door'.

Example 2

GO FOR THE WATER

> There was a brother and a sister one time, they were back in the west of Kerry. Oh and a very remote place altogether. So the water was that far away from them that they always used to be grumbling and grousing, the two of them, which of them would go for the water. They'd always come to the decision anyway that they'd have their little couple of verses and whoever'd stop first, they'd have to go for the water. So they'd sit at both sides of the fire anyway and there was two little hobs that time, there used be no chairs, only two hobs. One would be sitting at one side and one at the other side and maybe Jack would have his doodeen, d'you know, that's what they used to call a little clay pipe, and Jack'd sing:

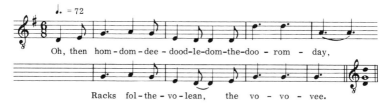

Oh, then hom-dom-dee-doodle-dom-the-doo - rom - day,

Racks fol-the-vo-lean, the vo - vo - vee.

So now it would go over to Mary:
[sung] 'Oh, then. . .' etc.

So back to Jack again:
[sung] 'Oh, then. . .' etc.

So they'd keep on like that from morning maybe until night and who'd
ever stop would have to go for the water. So there was an old man
from Tralee, anyway, and he was driving a horse and sidecar, they'd be
calling it a taxi now. He'd come on with his horse and sidecar maybe
from a railway station or some place and they'd hire him to drive them
back to the west of Dingle. So bejay, he lost his way anyway, and 'twas
the only house for another four or five miles, so in he goes to enquire
what road he'd to take. And when he landed inside the door, he said,
How do I get to Ballyferriter from here? And Mary said:
[sung] 'Oh, then. . .', etc.

So over he went, 'What's wrong with that one? She must be mad or
something.' And over to the old man, he said, 'How do I get to
Ballyferriter from here?'
[sung] 'Oh, then. . .', etc.

He go back over to Mary and he was getting the same results off Mary;
and back to Jack again. Now this old man, he wouldn't take a chance
and go off without getting the information where the place was. So he
catches hold of Mary and starts tearing her around the place, 'Show
me the road to Ballyferriter!', shaking her, pushing her and pulling her
and everything.
[sung] 'Oh, then. . .', etc.

and he kept pulling her and tearing her around the place and he
pucking her and everything. 'Oh, Jack,' says she, 'will you save me?'
'Oh, I will, Mary, but you'll have to go for the water!'

Travelling life has undergone radical changes in the last thirty or
forty years. Changes in farming methods and the development of
materials such as plastic have meant that travellers can no longer make
a living at tinsmithing, and the mechanisation of farming has led to the
almost total disappearance of the travelling horse and donkey dealer.
Once the travellers were welcome visitors in rural areas for their
manual skills and also for their abilities as singers, musicians, and
storytellers. One farmer in the west of Ireland told us how, when they

were in his area, he would go off with them for a week at a time 'just to pick up a few songs'. Music once played a vital part in Irish rural life. In parts of County Clare, so important was it that, when the floors were being laid in newly built cottages, an old iron pot or kettle, or an animal's skull was placed beneath a flagstone in a central spot in the kitchen (the main room), so that when that spot was danced on, the sound would reverberate. These cavities were known as 'battering pots'.

The decline in the musical tradition in Ireland has played a strong part in the fact that the communication between the settled and travelling communities has all but disappeared. It should be remembered that the death of these musical traditions was not entirely from natural causes as it was elsewhere in the British Isles. It was helped on its way by the combined efforts of the Catholic clergy, who objected to the country house and crossroads dances on the grounds that they were detrimental to the morals of the youth of Ireland, and the Irish Government's Public Dance Halls Act of 1936 which required all public dancing to be licensed under conditions laid down by the District Justices. Thanks to the isolation of the travelling community and, until recently, the immunity from outside cultural influences such as television and radio, singing and storytelling survived as living traditions right into the 1970s. When we first started recording travellers in 1973, it was still possible to go back to the site after the pub closed and become involved in singing sessions around an open fire. The development of the portable, battery-powered television virtually destroyed this in a matter of a couple of years. Nevertheless, it is still possible to find travellers with large repertoires and considerable singing skills. Mikeen, at the age of fifty, is one of the oldest singers we have recorded to date, the majority being between twenty and forty years old.

Travellers have had a considerable influence on the musical and singing traditions of Ireland, both by distributing the songs on ballad sheets and by carrying them and the tunes from area to area. Their migrations to and fro across the Irish Sea are among the reasons why it is possible to find songs in the repertories of Galway, Clare, and Donegal singers that are usually associated with England and Scotland, and vice versa.

Singers like Mikeen have made a tremendous contribution to the singing traditions of the past and are still able to assist us in our understanding of those traditions. Apart from the older songs, they have been instrumental in preserving songs that have come into being during their own lifetimes and have gained very little, if any, currency outside the communities in which they were conceived. Such a song is the final example recorded in Spring 1976, concerning a Roscommon farmer who, on reaching the age of seventy-one, decides that he should marry and so advertises for a wife in the local paper, with unforeseen consequences.

Example 3

FLOWERY NOLAN

Michael McCarthy
Spring 1976

Oh, he lived up-on the Stokestown Road, con-ven-ient to Ar-phin,

A man called Flow'-ry No - lan, a ter-ror to all men;

He reached the age of se-ven-ty-one and he thought it himself it was time

For to go and get a mis-sus, his wedding 'twould be no crime.

Major variations:

v. 2 Oh sev-eral maids came of-fer to him and from them all he fled,

Ex-cept one young fair maid, her for-tune was ra-ther high...

v. 4 I lived all a-lone for se-ven-ty-one and I'll lie a-lone to-night.

Oh, he lived upon the Stokestown Road, convenient to Arphin,
A man called Flowery Nolan, a terror to all men;
He reached the age of seventy-one and he thought it himself it was
    time
For to go and get a missus, his wedding 'twould be no crime.

Oh, several maids came offer to him and from them all he fled,
Except one young fair maid, her fortune was rather high,
So he took and he married this young fair maid to be his wedded
    wife.

Oh, the wedding it lasted two nights and one day till one night going in
    to bed,
Oh, Flowery turned all to his wife and these are the words he said;
'You think you are my wedded wife but I'll tell you you're not,
You are only but my serving maid and better is your lot.

Oh, there is two beds in my bedroom and take the one to the right,
I lived all alone for seventy-one and I'll lie alone tonight.'

Oh, when Mrs Nolan heard those words she thought her husband
    queer,
Oh, packing up her belongings and from him she went away;
She tramped the road to her father's house and 'tis there she did
    remain,
And then all the men in the Stokestown Road wouldn't get her back
    again.

So now all ye pretty young fair maids, take a warning take by me,
Never marry an old man or 'tis sorry you will be,
Never marry an old man until you're fed up of your life,
Or then you'll be coming home again like Flowery Nolan's wife.

He was an old bachelor for years, he used to be always talking about
getting married, but when he made up his mind to get married, he'd
wait until the next year, and the next year, and he'd go on like that till
he was seventy-one years of age. The farmers round told him it would
do no harm to have someone to look after him, so he advertised in the
paper for a wife; it was a joke more than anything else. All the lads
around the parish were more blackguards than anything else, so a lot
of the girls came around pulling his leg, letting on they were going to
marry him. This one really meant it. Out of all her jokes, till she got
the dirty turn-out.

Arthur Howard   *Photo by Ian Russell*

CONTEXT AND CONTENT:
A STUDY OF THE REPERTOIRES OF ARTHUR HOWARD*

Ian Russell

[Arthur] had in his repertoire, he had a book and he'd songs for
Sunday school dos, songs for ladies' evenings, and he'd songs for
gentlemen's evenings, and whatever function he were attending he
used to look those up, you see, and just go through them. (Wright
Cooper)

He'd always semp to pick 'em just right. (William Nobel)[1]

When Arthur Howard died on 27 August 1982 at the age of 79, it was a
sad loss not only for his family and friends but also to his farming
acquaintances, sheepkeepers, the National Farmers' Union (NFU), the
hunting fraternity, the local pubs, old people's homes, folksong clubs,
and the community at large. Arthur did not suffer the gradual decline
brought on by old age and it was not until the last few months before he
died that his faculties became impaired. Up until that time he was as
active and outgoing as a man half his age. When Yorkshire Television
filmed him for their programme about the Shepherds' Society,[2] the
producer commented to me that the Duchess of Harewood, the subject
of another film, did not have a diary half as full as Arthur had. He was a
very busy man, such that I would have to arrange our meetings weeks in
advance.

More often than not, when Arthur went out in the evening he would
sing or recite, and, if he stayed at home, singing was his hobby and
learning new songs his preoccupation. Understandably, few traditional

*This paper was given at the 'Fieldwork in Folklore' Conference at the
University of Sheffield, 19 November 1983, and accompanied by tape-recorded
examples. I am particularly grateful to William Noble, Michael Pickering, and
Vic Gammon for the information and comments they have provided, and to
Marjorie Wood for her support and permission to reproduce her father's
songs.

singers in England, if any, could match such dedication. It is rare these days to encounter a singer who performs so regularly (outside the context of the folksong revival) and for whom the songs have such importance. It is because Arthur's songs were so meaningful to him and functioned in so many ways that a closer examination of the performance contexts and the contents of his repertoire is particularly rewarding.

At this point it would be helpful to establish the resources available to this study and to distinguish the various contexts. At home Arthur sang for his family, including his grandchildren, and for visitors and friends; he also sang for himself and from 1976-80 systematically recorded over 250 songs as a legacy for his children. From 1980-83 I visited Arthur at home and recorded about 180 songs and recitations as well as conversation totalling nearly a hundred hours of tape. Arthur had in his possession eight handwritten family songbooks plus a large quantity of commercially printed songsheets, sheet music, and song books. He also had several miscellaneous sheets, typed, cyclostyled, or handwritten, containing the words of a song or verse.

From this amount of information it ought to be possible to establish what songs were performed at home, what songs were sung for visitors, for family, for children, and for a visiting researcher, as well as the repertoire inherited from his parents.

Outside the home, the contexts in which Arthur would sing included the Shepherds' Meet, the NFU gatherings, the hunt suppers, Saturday or Sunday night at the pub, old people's parties, and, in later years, Thursday night at the local folksong club. When these contexts have been investigated with reference to representatives from the various groups there should be sufficient evidence to support or refute the proposition of this paper: that Arthur would select his songs according to the company he was with and that this selection implied not one repertoire, nor even two—active and passive[3]—but several. The extent to which such repertoires may be overlapping, coincidental, or distinct will also need to be discussed.

One context not included above is that of work. This is not in itself surprising as the work of a sheepfarmer does not involve, on a regular basis, any particular repetitive and rhythmic task, such as handmilking or the weaving and 'waulking' of cloth. In such a context a song might be used to relieve the tedium. Arthur Howard was not alone in this absence in his repertoire. The Sussex shoemaker, Henry Burstow of Horsham, a prodigious singer who died in 1916, listed few, if any, songs relating to his trade out of the 420 items that he sang.[4] This contrasts with a Hebridean setting where James Ross notes that much of Nan MacKinnon's repertoire consisted of work songs:

> A large number of songs were connected with communal activity of an occupational kind.[5]

He also notes the importance of 'ritualistic songs' such as those performed to cure illness or as part of a New Year custom. If Arthur had such repertoires, he certainly never admitted to them. Whereas James Ross was describing a song tradition closely integrated into the working life of a community, Arthur's tradition was largely related to leisuretime and was predominantly an individualised form of entertainment. That is not to say that Arthur did not sing about his work but rather that an opportunity to do this was not devoted to a particularly appropriate group of songs. In fact, the occasion would be used to memorise and practise songs later performed in one or more of the settings noted above. A series of incidents that occurred following the release of his gramophone record illustrate this. Several reporters such as the one from the *Daily Mail* interviewed Arthur in order to obtain interesting copy for their papers.[6] The *Mail*'s headline ran:

> Shepherd rounds up folk songs for the record

and began

> Evening on the moors of Hazlehead always echoed to the strain of that simple ballad 'It was night and the moon illuminated the sky'. Arthur Howard was humming a lullaby ... to his sheep.

The tabloid and local newspapers would also want a suitable photograph—suitable to their conception of what Arthur should represent. Thus they insisted on transporting him on to the moors where some sheep could be found. Arthur would then be required to perch on a bit of broken walling and sing, keeping the sheep in the shot. Arthur obliged but later confessed that he'd never sung *to* the sheep in his life. For a BBC 'Look North' feature, Arthur was required by the producer to sing as he tramped up the side of a moor towards a flock of sheep.[7] Arthur did his best, but the sheep took fright and ran away, while Arthur got short of breath and had to stop. The media's concept of what Arthur's singing context should be was a complete concoction. Although he attempted to dispel their illusion, they chose to ignore him and Arthur, flattered by the limelight, politely did their bidding.

Before presenting an account of Arthur's singing contexts, it would be useful to summarise his background and the environment in which he was brought up. Arthur was born on Christmas Eve 1902 at Mount Farm, Holme, some three to four miles into the hills above Holmfirth, and just below Holme Moss where the television mast now stands. At that time the landscape must have looked very different. Such upland farms were many and well maintained with their neatly walled fields of rough pasture, hay, oats, and potatoes. Today, as the direct result of the policy of water authorities and government, most of the farms are gone, the land is depopulated, walls are dilapidated, fields have reverted to rush, heather, bracken, and bilberry. A patchwork of cultivation has given way to the blackness of conifer plantations and the steely greyness of vast acres of reservoirs.

The Howards and the Haighs (his grandmother's family) had farmed the land, kept sheep, and spun and woven cloth in the neighbourhood of Holme since before the land was enclosed and the first records kept. From these times their economy and lifestyle had been twofold:

> Me Grandfather Howard built Mount for a weaving shed. It was all
> windows upstairs. There were four handlooms and a twisting frame,
> and, of course, little spinning wheels and that sort of thing, and what
> they called *wuzzers*. They used to put their bobbins in a hole in the
> wall about the size of an eggcup, after they'd steamed them, and turn
> this handle and *wuzz* them round to dry. (T)

Arthur was the fourth of six children, four girls and two boys, and with a grandmother living in, there was always a full house. Arthur's father, Haigh, had a full-time job as shepherd and gamekeeper for the Shepley brewers, Seth Seniors and Son, and, because of this, all the farmwork had to be done in the early mornings, evenings, and at weekends. The two women of the house managed the stock. Arthur recalled: 'It were mainly bed and work then', but added 'There was allus something going off, always plenty of jokes'. (T) He enjoyed school especially painting and craftwork, and his watercolour portraits of wildlife are still treasured.

Predictably, money was tight and the farm could not support them all, so he started work as an apprentice at nearby Rakes Mill. He was never fond of the work:

> I practically went through the mill. I were *reachin'* in, *twistin'* in,
> *yeldin'* in, weavin', did a spell at warehouse ... I start at half past six
> in the morning until half past five at night. I'd two miles to walk each

way . . . Time we'd milked an' one thing and another, it were time to go to bed, and you didn't need any rocking, you know! (T)

Both Arthur's parents were singers. His mother had a somewhat different repertoire from his father; she specialised in sentimental and soldiers' songs (her father had been a soldier) and she came from a different district, Tintwizzle. Arthur's father had written out many of his songs in books for himself and latterly for his children. He was also the village musician for country dancing:

> Me father used to play for dancing and when we'd come home from mill at night, he'd say, 'What's latest Arthur?' and I used to sing 'em over to him and he'd play 'em ont' melodeon and then same night play 'em for dancing. (T)

In his early twenties Arthur gave up millwork to become part-time village electrician with responsibility for maintaining the local hydro-electric generator. At 26 he got married to a nursemaid and took over Mount Farm from his father. Mount was a mixed farm. Only in 1941 when he took over Pikenaze Farm in the Woodhead Pass did Arthur become exclusively a sheep farmer and this 2,500 acre moorland is still farmed by his son, Rider. His daughter, Marjorie, and her husband, John Wood, run the farm at Hazlehead which Arthur bought and lived in from 1960 until his death. Arthur's wife had died in 1965.

My first encounter with Arthur was at the Shepherds' Meet of the Dunford Bridge Shepherds' Society on 5 November 1972. This gathering is termed the 'mother meeting' because the marks for all the other societies or liberties in the district including Hayfield, Rishworth, Holmfirth, Meltham, Marsden, Derwent, Penistone, Bradfield, and others are decided there. The meet is held twice yearly to see to the return of strays and to settle disputes, but my interest and I suspect that of most of the company was in the social occasion—the dinner and the evening singsong that followed. For the last thirty years of his life Arthur had seen it as part of his job as chairman of the society to act as MC for the entertainment.

The Stanhope Arms at Dunford Bridge is a late-Victorian imposing pub built to withstand the bleak winters and to accommodate travellers from the railway and salesmen, or migrant workmen from the reservoirs. The concert room is really two rooms with a large partition folded back between them, separated from the bar, and it is here that the shepherds dine and spend their evening.[8] Before motorised transport, the summer meeting had been an excuse for a week's holiday or 'razzle' conveniently placed between clipping and haytime. By the 1970s, the special atmosphere of a holiday was still in evidence but the number of shepherds attending dwindled to about thirty.

> It isn't as much now as it used to be in my younger days when I was chairman in the beginning. There aren't the sort of social evenings anywhere in the district that there used to be, because they used to make their own amusement. Now it's all telly and wireless. They wouldn't know how to start to make an evening of that sort. There's a lot of old characters who have died out. There are still some left and some growing up. They're different to what they used to be. Life isn't as rough as it used to be. You can't get hardly any young ones, just a few, who get up and sing; but at my time of day it used to be practically everyone that could sing a song. Nowadays you only get a few. The others all come, they'd listen all night, but they won't do a turn on their own. It's hard work if there's just three or four entertaining a roomful. Before you could call on a dozen or more.
> (T)

Nonetheless, in 1972 about seven singers took to the floor, and the repertoire included thirty-three songs and recitations, which are listed in Appendix 1. Of these items, Arthur performed nineteen, fourteen in chorus and five on his own. The evening commenced with a piano medley and the first song was 'Gossip John' which Arthur prompted. 'Gossip John' is perhaps the best known of a group of songs that are performed in chorus by all the principal singers as well as most of the 'audience' in the room. It is always an extremely animated rendition that featured here four singers, Arthur Howard, John Kaye, Ian Siswick, and Peter (?), who typically would stand side by side. The singing is raucously and rowdily declaimed, and great play is made of gesture and expression. The song is also punctuated by syncopation, asides, and sound effects (the mooing of a cow), most of which are as much a part of the performance as the lyrics and the piano accompaniment.[9]

There are several reasons why such a song should recommend itself to this style of performance. The sense of bawdry and the risqué humour have obvious appeal. The frivolities of the melody allow for both extemporisation and simple harmonization. The extremely corny humour is clearly relished, but for motives that are far from transparent. (I could spend time here discussing why an essentially town-based parody of the country yokel, like 'Richard of Taunton Dean', should be so popular among country men, and how this apparent self-parody functions, but I will reserve that digression for elsewhere.)[10] Suffice it to say that, with the barest analysis, it can be confidently stated that 'Gossip John' is a favourite chorus song.

Arthur's contribution to the performance is not discernible from the recording, but it should be noted that he prompted the song, fetched the other singers to their feet, performed all the verses, gestures, and the important aside—(after 'They're lots more verses to this song, but we're not bound to sing them' ...) 'They're not fit to 'ear!'—and prompted his fellow singers when they hesitated; but because his voice lacked the power of the others, he is largely inaudible on the recording.

During the course of the evening, the flow of performance was several times interrupted. A singer, who had been lined up to perform, failed to return from the bar; another, reluctant to perform, made excuses. In such circumstances Arthur sensed the lull and would quickly come to the rescue with an appropriate contribution. Such were the circumstances when he performed the monologue which he prefaced with:

> Well, we'll have to tell you some Bible stories. It's a big book but not
> big enough to take all t'details of 'How Noah saved t'ark' ... (T)

Sadly the tape recorder will save only sound and even then, unlike the human ear which is able to home in on one particular element, records indiscriminately. Unfortunately, there is no visual record of Arthur's monologue performance, particularly his use of gesture and his facial expression; though we can summarise that it was usually a relaxed and unselfconscious delivery, untheatrical and low-key, but hardly deadpan. Typically he would keep one eye on the listener watching for a reaction, for the involuntary smile that would surely crack the stoniest of faces.

For much of the evening, Arthur's role was twofold: to get other singers on to their feet and to keep the entertainment going. We have heard already how he allowed others to take the lead in the chorus contributions. 'Mrs Olroyd' (see Example 1) emphasises other important qualities, characteristic of many of the 'come-all-ye' items: dialect is predominant to the level of carricature, there are frequent in-jokes, while great play is made of suggestive and punning lyrics. Moreover, performance is seen as an obligation: 'Have we to do "Mrs Olroyd"?'.

The other chorus songs in which Arthur took part are indicated in Appendix 1. It can easily be seen that some of these would readily follow

Example 1

MRS OLROYD

Arthur Howard
and others at the Stanhope Arms
6 November 1972

Transcribed by Ian Russell

So I've just come round to ask you Miss-es Ol - royd

Can you feel owt like rain?'

I'm a right bad judge o't weather and if e'er I go away,
If I leave ma top coit at whome I'll bet it rains all t'day
Wife says to me, 'Sam, dost tha think, this weather's bound to last?'
I says, 'Now lass, tha maunt ask me, tha knows me of the past.'
She said, 'If I thought it war' we'd set off for a day.
Go round to t'widow Olroyd. I'll tell thee what to say—

[Chorus]
'Na then Misses Olroyd, can you feel owt?
If you can I'd like to know;
For they say that there's a big breeze on at Blackpool
And I thought you'd like the blow.
They say that you can tell when t'weather's changing
By the twitching of your rheumatic pain,
So I've just come round to ask you Misses Olroyd
Can you feel owt like rain?'

Mrs Olroyd said, 'You all get off, there'll be no rain today.'
And varry soon at Blackpool, we enjoyed both breeze and spray.
We 'adn't been there varry long before me wife yells out,
'Sithee! Sam, there's Mrs Olroyd?' and there war' without a doubt,
She sat on a young chap's knee feeling bright and gay;
I felt that flabbergasted I couldn't help but say—
[Chorus]

We landed back at Stanhope just about eleven at neet,
And as there were a wa' on we couldn't 'ave a leet.
We roamed down Spider's Alley, we could norther stand nor sit
When we 'eard somebody shouting, 'Mrs Olroyd, up a bit!'
Mrs Olroyd gave a yell as though she was in pain;
She'd planted on a wasps' nest and we asked her once again—
[Chorus]

a similar performance pattern—'Old King Cole', 'Nutting Song', and 'Johnny Bugger'. It is harder to accept that 'The Bold Gendarmes', or 'Joe the Carrier's Lad', or even 'The Rockwood Hounds' achieved such active involvement from the participants, but each did, for the humour was essentially in the manner of their performance.

In Arthur's other function, to provide continuity, we can see a second set of items that seem to represent a more personal choice. Yet it would be wrong to consider that any of these songs or monologues were in any sense strange to the context, for all were chosen as the result of requests. It would have been no surprise to any of the other singers to have been told that Arthur knew all the songs performed that evening, after all they had mostly learnt the songs from his singing; but they were probably unaware that this sample of the repertoire had been largely prescribed by Arthur. These were the songs that he considered most suitable to the Shepherds' Meet. If he had not been directly responsible for prompting their performance that night, he had certainly done so in the past, by performing them himself or by setting the pattern of what was acceptable. For most other singers, such chorus songs might acount for more than half their repertoire, but for Arthur it was less than one tenth.

In many respects the singsongs that followed a day's hunting were (and are) very similar to the Shepherds' Meet. At both gatherings the humour was raucous and bawdy, while participation and chorus songs were greatly favoured. Almost any such evening in the 1960s would feature Arthur, in the company of his elder brother James, and Frank Hinchliffe (of Holme) singing 'Gossip John', 'The Castle Hill Anthem' ('Pleasant and Delightful'), and 'Mrs Olroyd'. Known as the three brothers (Frank was always mistakenly thought to be a third brother), they would perform standing side by side, just as the singers did at Dunford Bridge. Unfortunately, I never witnessed such an evening and we are grateful to Dave Bland's recording of the singing of the Holme Valley Beagles, made in 1972-73, for a detailed, eye-witness account.[11]

Just as Arthur was behind most of the songs performed at the Shepherds' Meet, this was also true of the Hunt. Whilst individuals would specialise in one particular hunting song, Arthur had at least 23 that he could call on if required (see Appendix 2), or if the particular singer were missing. However, it was usual in such circumstances for Arthur to pass over this distinctly hunting repertoire and choose items to lighten the proceedings. Although it was Fred Woodcock, the pianist, that kept the singing going and Arthur was often reluctant to sing first, his role was not markedly different from that at the Shepherds' Meet. Nor was it a coincidence that the only risquévr song among the hunting items should have become the one most associated with Arthur, 'The Christmas Goose'.[12]

Not surprisingly there is a close correlation between the repertoire of songs that Arthur sang at the Saturday night pub singsong with those humorous and 'come-all-ye' items performed by him at the Shepherds' Meet and the Hunt social. For that reason I will move on to consider Arthur's role and his repertoire at an old people's home and that performed by him at folksong clubs and festivals.

Will Noble regularly accompanied Arthur to an old people's home at Penistone for their Christmas party. Will drew my attention to several points about Arthur's performance; Arthur had no trouble choosing songs that appealed to this senior audience; whilst sentimental songs were much in evidence, this did not prevent Arthur from including humorous items and often risquévr ones as well; Will heard Arthur perform songs that were unfamiliar from his knowledge of Arthur at the Hunt socials. Typical sentimental songs that were sung were 'When We Went to School Together', 'Where is Now the Merry Party?', 'When the Fields are White with Daisies', and 'The Boys of the Old Brigade'. This choice reflected both Arthur's mother's taste for songs as well as the requests of his audience. The humour Arthur chose, as Will remembers, was particularly suited to the occasion. 'The Egg' parodies twelve songs, most of which would be instantly recognisable to a senior audience. Thus far I have identified 'Maxwelton Braes', 'The Boys of the Old Brigade', 'Poor Old Joe', 'Mademoiselle from Armentieres', 'In and Out the Window', 'The Minstrel Boy', 'The Bay of Biscay', 'Excelsior', 'Tarpaulin Jacket', and 'Rule Britannia'.[13] Certainly 'The Egg' is representative of Arthur's choice, but as yet it has not been possible to compile a comprehensive list of this repertoire.

On Thursday nights in the 1970s, Arthur regularly visited the folksong club at the Cherry Tree Inn, High Hoyland. He also sang on several occasions at a Monday night folksong club in Wakefield. Two other engagements at which he performed are particularly of interest. In September 1976 he was one of four or five traditional singers invited to entertain the members of the Society for Folklife Studies at a social gathering organised in the Street of York Castle Museum. One of Arthur's last public performances was given at the Downs Festival of

Example 2

COME ON, COME ON

Arthur Howard
15 September 1980

Transcribed by Ian Russell

Now, one fine day in the month of May when the sun did brightly shine,

And hav-ing lots of time I called of a pal of mine;

We'd no i - dea where we should steer to spend an hour or so,

Till at last we both made up our minds to the ra - ces we would go.

In half an hour we stood up - on the course,

All our mon-ey we put up - on a horse;

It came in first, I stood up - on my 'ead,

Slows

I threw my hat in - to the air and to my pals I said

(Chorus) 'Come on, come on, let's go and draw our tin!

If all works well be - fore to-night, we'll blow the whole lot in;

We rushed to where, we'd made our bets and found the book - ie gone,

Me pal says, 'Well, I'll go to hell! Come on, come on!'

Now one fine day in the month of May when the sun did brightly shine,
And having lots of time I called on a pal of mine;
We'd no idea where we should steer to spend an hour or so,
Till at last we both made up our minds to the races we would go.
In half an hour we stood upon the course,
All our money we put upon a horse;
It came in forst, I stood upon my 'ead,
I threw my hat into the air and to my pals I said—

'Come on, come on, let's go and draw our tin!
If all works well before tonight, we'll blow the whole lot in.'
We rushed to where, we'd made our bets and found the bookie gone,
Me pal says, 'Well, I'll go to hell! Come on, come on!'

Last summertime I went away upon my holiday,
My heart was light and gay for a month I meant to stay,
And being fond of bathing down in the briny sea,
One day I just peeled off my clothes beneath a shady tree.
How I enjoyed myself, there's no-one knows,
When I came out someone had pinched my clothes;
Just then I spied two ladies passing by;
I tried to hide behind myself when I heard one of them cry—

'Come on, come on! Why are you standing there?'
Said Lil to Lou, 'I'm shocked at you. What is it makes you stare?'
I felt myself turn black and blue, when I heard the youngest one
Say, 'Deary me, there's nowt to see! Come on, come on!'

I remember yet, I'll ne'er forget when first I took a wife
To share my happy life, it caused me joy and strife.
My pals all came to wish me luck which filled me with delight;
I'll ne'er forget the fun we had on that eventful night.
My pals all drank till they could drink no more;
Some were blind and rolled upon the floor.
The clock struck three, I danced with all the girls,
Forgetting I was newly wed, I shouted to my pals—

'Come on, come on! It's far too late to roam.
Be good, me boys, don't make a noise! It's time we all went home.'
I was looking for my lodgings when my darling wife said, 'John!
We're newly wed, let's go to bed! Come on, come on!'

Traditional Singing at Hermitage during the weekend of 22-23 May 1982.

Arthur's choice of material showed awareness of the extent to which his audience was a captive one and of the atmosphere in which he was performing. It is ironic that a man who never himself drank alcoholic drinks should be so dependent on the drinking habits of others and spend so much time in their drinking haunts. As far as the non-drinking venue of an old people's home was concerned, Arthur took advantage of the situation to perform songs that were personal, that required an attentive audience, and were without rowdy chorus songs that had appealed to his wife. Even more attentive were some of the audiences of folksong revivalists that Arthur encountered. Thus in the Street to a rather highbrow audience he sang 'Rosemary Lane', 'Polly Oliver', and 'The Sucking Pig', which were all politely received. However, he failed in his attempt to enliven this rather stuffed-shirt company with the humour of 'The Egg', which was quite wasted on them, or the outrageousness of 'Piddling Pete', which they found somewhat embarrassing.

Between 1976 and the Downs Festival in 1982 Arthur's regular visits to folksong clubs gave him a more relaxed perspective on how to react in the company of these largely middle-class, student, and town-oriented groups. He found subtle humour worked in such company; he found they listened intently to long narrative songs and occasionally he would include just one; but usually he preferred to dissipate the tensions of such sessions with humour. Few of Arthur's songs went down as well as his opening one at the Downs Festival, 'Come On, Come On!' (see Example 2, above).

It would be fair to say that by the time he performed at the Downs Festival, his folksong club repertoire had a lot in common with his usual pub singing, though it is possible to pick out about half the items that were specific to this setting (and these are double-asterisked in Appendix 3). Some of these were his versions of songs popularised on the folk scene such as 'It was down at Albert Square' which Arthur knew as 'Away down to Pomona'. He remarked , 'It's not *your* tune but I don't know another'. On one occasion I asked Arthur if he'd ever tried singing his rather unusual version of 'Fathom the Bowl' at a folksong club. He nodded but added that it had proved impossible to go through with as the audience wouldn't sing his tune. Another song, 'Pretty Flowers', Arthur had very little time for, but whenever he performed at folksong clubs it was always requested, because of its inclusion on the Holme Valley Beagles' L.P.[14] The folksong clubs were also a rich hunting ground for him. While it is true that he tended to stick to the same songs when performing at the clubs, he was always listening for possible new additions. In fact, he didn't have a very high opinion of some of the singers at folksong clubs and remarked:

> They mostly sing them to these twangers [guitars], they've all same tune practically all the way through. Then once, now and again, you get a decent song. (T)

Once found he would attempt a trade and if this was impractical he might make a tape recording. Examples of songs learnt at a folksong club and subsequently performed are 'The Champion Muckspreader', 'The Unlucky Duck', 'Twice Daily', 'The Black Velvet Band', 'The Wild Mountain Thyme', 'Jones's Ale', and 'As I was Going to Aylesbury' (see Appendix 4).

Arthur also wrote out the words of songs that he intended to learn. The source for these songs was not always the folksong club itself, but rather that singers at the club would loan Arthur published song collections or direct him to a particular volume such as Bob Copper's *A Song for Every Season* and Frank Kidson's *Traditional Tunes*, which he borrowed from the library.[15]

In terms of size of total repertoire much the largest part was kept for domestic use. In 1980 when Joseph, our son, was five years old, we visited Arthur. He sat him on his knee and sang to him without any prompting 'I Bought Three Pigs at Marsden Fair' and 'Old Jepson Brown'.[16] Two other favourites that Arthur had sung regularly to his grandchildren, when they were little, were 'Little Jack a Poor Sweep Boy' and 'Razor Rig' (see Example 3,). He also recited rhymes to them, such as:

> Two little pigs to market went,
> Their names were Paul and Patience;
> They were both sold and both sent
> To different destinations.
>
> And as the two were dragged apart
> Paul said in soothing tones,
> 'Don't cry! We'll meet again, sweetheart,
> I feel it in my bones'.

> And they did meet again one day,
> Paul hadn't been mistaken;
> He was a sausage on my plate
> And Patience was the bacon! (T)

The largest two repertoires of songs identified here relate to his performance to me, on the one hand, and to his family through his own tape recordings, on the other. All my fieldwork recordings and Arthur's recordings were made at Saville House Farm, Hazlehead, in Arthur's cramped kitchen/living room. In the centre, in front of the fire, was the table which served as his desk, filing cabinet, as well as eating place. His archives were in a shoe box. At the back of the room in the corner was a stack of shepherd's sticks, a large dresser with a few carved and stuffed animals, a sunken armchair, and the kitchen sink. The room was typically cluttered with boxes, papers, books, piles of letters, magazines, and newspapers. He lived in one end of the rugged old farmhouse while his daughter, Marjorie, and her family had the rest. To me he would sing seated in his armchair turning slightly towards me, his eyes twinkling as he relished his song. With a wave of his hand he would warn me of when he was ready to start and finish. Typical of the items recorded during such sessions is 'Adieu, my Lovely Nance' (see Example 4, p. 48).

An impressive list of about fifty items that Arthur sang for me were not, as far as I know, performed outside the home (see Appendix 5). While it may be that many of these songs fall within the 'passive' repertoire,[17] that is not to say that the songs did not carry a great deal of meaning but rather that their only context was that of the hearthside, and their only audience was that of Arthur himself or, perhaps, a close friend. The repertoire combines early nineteenth-century broadsides with mid-to-late Victorian sentimental parlour ballads, such that it's hard to identify any part of the repertoire that would not have been sung a hundred years ago. The selection as such represents a legacy, the songs that Arthur's parents and grandparents thought deserved to be passed on.

Arthur in turn passed on a legacy of songs to his children in a form far more accessible than that used by his parents: he systematically tape-recorded over 250. I have listed in Appendix 6 only those songs that have not been noted or recorded outside the home and that are not included in the other appendixes. The list is quite remarkable not only because there are over a hundred items, but rather because there is clear evidence of new songs constantly being learnt from popular sources, for

Example 3

OLD RAZOR RIG

Arthur Howard
1 September 1980

Transcribed by Ian Russell

Old Razor Rig was as rare a pig as ever your did see;
His ears were long an' is legs were strong an' as crook'd as they could be;
'E had one eye and only one, which made 'im look sae queer,
And 'is nose it turned up at the end and 'e grinned from ear to ear.

To me fol-la-dol-lay, fol-la-dol-lay, fol-la-dol-ler-a-lay,
Fol-la-dol-lay, fol-la-dol-lay, fol-la-dol-ler-a-lay!

Now, when the butcher killed this pig, 'e might 'a lost his life,
For 'e was up to the knees in blood an' 'e called for a longer knife,
And when they come to oppen him, the like afore were never,
To think 'at a pig like Razor Rig should dee without a liver!
[laughs in chorus]

Example 4

ADIEU, MY LOVELY NANCY

Arthur Howard
27 January 1981

Transcribed by Ian Russell

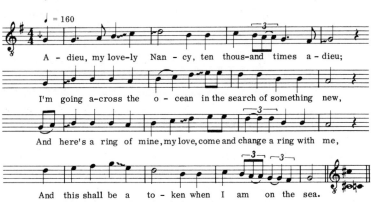

A - dieu, my love-ly Nan - cy, ten thous-and times a - dieu;

I'm going a-cross the o - cean in the search of something new,

And here's a ring of mine, my love, come and change a ring with me,

And this shall be a to - ken when I am on the sea.

Adieu, my lovely Nancy, ten thousand times adieu;
I'm going across the ocean in the search of something new,
And here's a ring of mine, my love, come and change a ring with me,
And this shall be a token when I am on the sea.

When I am on the sea, my love, you'll know not where I am,
But letters I will write to you from every foreign land;
With the secrets of my heart, my love, and the best of my goodwill,
For let my body lie where it will, my heart lies with you still.

There's a heavy storm arising, see how it gathers round!
While we poor souls on the ocean wide are fighting for the crown.
There is nothing to protect us, love, or to keep us from the cold,
On the ocean wide where we must bide like jolly seamen bold.

There are tinkers, tailors, and shoemakers lie snoring fast asleep,
While we, poor souls, on the ocean wide are ploughing through the deep;
Our officers commanding us and them we must obey,
Expecting every moment for to get cast away.

But when the wars are over, there'll be peace on every shore.
We'll return to our wives and families and the girls that we adore.
We will call for liquor merrily and spend our money free,
And when our money is all gone, we'll boldly go to sea.

example Chuck Berry's 'My Dingaling', Jim Reeves's 'I Love You Just Because', and Rolf Harris's 'Two Little Boys'.

Roger D. Abraham in the Afterword to *A Singer and her Songs: Almeda Riddle's Book of Ballads* discusses the question of 'appropriateness'.[18] He noted that Granny Riddle would be pressed at Folk Festivals to sing her version of 'Go Tell Aunt Nancy' and that she would be reluctant to do so. To her the song was inappropriate: it should have been performed for children. (Abrahams also noted that Granny Riddle avoided obscene songs and dialogue courtship songs.) Certainly there is ample evidence in Arthur's singing that the same criterion of 'appropriateness' was at work in his decision to choose his material according to the setting.

Although this study, for practical reasons, fails to be comprehensive and the data could be subjected to much more rigorous analyses, it is nonetheless possible to reach firm conclusions from what has been presented here. In the case of Arthur Howard, there is clear evidence to show that context exerted a considerable influence on what he performed. Even his close friends and relatives, while they were aware of a process of selection being in operation, were quite unaware of large parts of Arthur's repertoire because they were unfamiliar with all the contexts in which he performed. Certain songs were performed almost anywhere and form a common core, many others, however, were reserved for specific settings. Within the frame of English vernacular singing tradition, Arthur Howard was a prodigious performer with an extraordinary repertoire. Because of his appreciation of context, his responsiveness to his audience, and his ability to empathise, he has provided us with an understanding of the nature of some of the controls governing a singer's repertoire and the performance strategies brought to bear. Above all else, this paper has demonstrated that context is a vitally important area of research, that should not be overlooked or underrated by the fieldworker.

Appendix 1: Items performed at the social evening following the Shepherds' Meet, 5 November 1972 (in order of performance)

Gossip John **
Piddling Pete (recitation) *
Mrs Olroyd **
How Noah Saved the Ark
    (recitation) *
Johnnie Bugger **
Bold English Navvy
Barley Mow
Water Rattle (Hear the Nightingale
    Sing) **
Bold Gendarmes **
Village Pump **
Shortness of Sight
Farmer's Boy
A-Roving
Castle Hill Anthem (Pleasant and
    Delightful) **
Old King Cole **
Grandfather's Watch (parody) *

Nutting Song **
Horn of the Hunter **
Rose of Tralee
Old Shep
Twice Daily
Foggy Dew
Three Crows
Rockwood Hounds **
Put my Hand on Myself
Farmer's Boy
German Clockmender *
Joe the Carrier's Lad **
Diadem (All Hail the Power)
Cwm Rhondda (Bread of Heaven)
Deep Harmony (Jesus Shall Reign)
She'll be Coming Round the
    Mountain **
You'll Never Get to Heaven **

Items performed by Arthur on his own
**Items performed by Arthur with other singers*

Appendix 2: Hunting Songs performed at home for the fieldworker

Brown Hare of Whitebrook
Christmas Goose
Doctor Mack
Echoing Horn
Hounds are out
It's a Fine Hunting Day
It was near to Honley Town
Joe Bowman
John Peel
Master Smith Says to John
Monarch of the Woods
Old Snowball

Old Towler
On a Fine Hunting Morn
On the 30th of October
Rockwood Hounds
Royd Hunt
Scent was Good
Some Gentlemen Take Great
    Delight
Some Fifty Years Ago
Squire Frith
There's a Bright Rosy Morning

Appendix 3: Items performed at the Downs Festival of Traditional Singing, Hermitage, 22-23 May 1982 (in order of performance)

Come On, Come On **
Piddling Pete (recitation) *
Dogs' Party (recitation) *
Nutting Song *
I'm a Copper **
Ding-Dong *
Pace-Egg Song *
I Bought Three Pigs **
I'm a Happy Hearted Farmer's Lad
Champion Muckspreader *
Grandfather's Watch (parody) *
Gossip John *
Death of Poor Bill Brown
How Noah Saved the Ark
   (recitation) *
Jonah and the Grampus
   (recitation) *

Merry Mountain Child *
German Clockmender *
Market Gardener **
Away Down to Pomona **
Pratty Flowers *
Where do Flies Go? **
Grannie's Old Armchair
Back Home in Tennessee (parody)
Johnny Sands
Sonia Snell (recitation)
Show Me the Way to Go Home
   (parody)
Discontented Cow (recitation) *
Darkies' Sunday School *
Sucking Pig *

These items were also sung at the folksong club at the Cherry Tree Inn, High Hoyland plus
   Rolling in the Grass
   The Egg
**These items were performed exclusively at folksong clubs and festivals.*

Appendix 4: Items learnt as a result of contact with the Folksong Revival

Adieu my Lovely Nancy
   (extra verses) *
Ale Glorious Ale
As I was Going to Aylesbury
Biggest One in Bury *
Black Velvet Band
Champion Muck Spreader
Five-foot Flirt *
John Barleycorn *
Jone's Ale
Knocker-Upper's Song
Leaving of Liverpool *

Molecatcher *
O Good Ale *
Old Snowball (extra verses) *
Sweet Violets
Twankydillo *
Twice Daily
Uncle Joe's Mintballs
Unlucky Duck
White Cockade (extra verses) *
Wild Mountain Thyme
Yellow Handkerchief

These items have not been tape-recorded by me.

Appendix 5: Additional items performed at home to the fieldworker

Adieu my Lovely Nancy
Banks of Sweet Dundee
Bell Bottom Trousers
Bonny Grey
Daughter of Shame
Devil and the Farmer's Wife
Don't be Angry with me Dad
Father Dear Father Come Home
Female Cabin Boy
Garden Gate
Golden Glove
Grace Darling
Green is the Grave
Gypsy Girl
Home Once More
Irish Emigrant
I Stood in a Police Court
It is the Sorrows of a Poor Old Man
It's Hard to Part a Man and Wife
It was Night and the Moon
Jocky to the Fair
Just Before the Battle Mother
A Light in the Window
Marsden Moor Murders

Meet Me by Moonlight
Paddle your own Canoe
Parson of Puddle
Polly Oliver
Powder Monkey
Red White and Blue
Rosemary Lane
Sentenced to Death
Ship that Never Returned
Slave's Dream
Stowaway
Tarpaulin Jacket
Teddy O'Neil
There's an Egg for your Breakfast
This Life is a Difficult Riddle
'Tis Hard to Give Thee Hand
Where is Now the Merry Party?
Whistling Winds
When We Went to School Together
White Cockade
Wild Rover
Woodpecker
Young Recruit

Appendix 6: Items taped by Arthur for his family and not noted elsewhere

Afton Water
All through the Night
A-Roving
Ash Grove
Banks of Allan Water
Banks of Ohio
Bells of St Mary's
Beautiful Dreamer
Bless this House
Blue-tailed Fly
Boy's Best Friend
British Grenadiers
Burlington Bertie

Carolina Moon
Come Brush up me Boots
D-Day Dodgers
Drink to Me Only
Flower from Mother's Grave
Galway Bay
Genevieve
Good Old Jeff
Happy Days are Here Again
Happy Wanderer
Here's a Health unto his Majesty
Horsey Keep your Tail up
Holy City

Home on the Range
How Can You Buy Killarney?
If I had the Wings of an Eagle
I'll Take you Home Again Kathleen
I'll Walk Beside You
I Love You Just Because
In Between the Showers
Isle of Innisfree
I Wandered through the Village Tom
I Want to be Alone Mary Brown
Just Break the News to Mother
Just down the Lane over the Stile
Just a Dream of you Dear
Lay Him away on the Hillside
Let the Rest of the World Go By
Lily Marlene
Little Grey Home in the West
Little Old Log Cabin in the Lane
Loch Lomond
Long Long Trail A-Winding
Maggie
Maggie May
Mary of Argyl
Minstrel Boy
My Ain Folk
My Dingaling
Nellie at Ten Past Nine
Oh Barney Take me Home Again
Oh Charlie Take it Away
Oh Darling Do Say Yes
Old Rustic Bridge
Ole Faithful
Poor Lad He's Gone
Poor Old Joe
Pulling Hard against the Stream
Que Sera Sera
Riley's Cowshorn
Rocked in the Cradle of the Deep
Rocking Alone in her own Rocking
    Chair
Roly Poly Pudding

Romping in the Fields
Sailor Boy
Shenandoah
Side by Side
Silver Threads among the Gold
Smiling Through
Spinning Wheel
Stein Song
Strawberry Fair
Song that Reached my Heart
Sweet and Low
Teddy Bears' Picnic
There is a Tavern
The Girl I Left Behind Me
The Man who Broke the Bank at
    Monte Carlo
The Sunshine of your Smile
The Veteran
Thora
Thrashing Song
'Tis the Ring your Mother Wore
'Tis of a Brisk Young Butcher
Tom Bowling
Toy Drum Major
Two Little Girls in Blue
Two Lovely Black Eyes
Wait Till the Clouds Roll by
Waratah
Waltzing Matilda
We Must Have One More Yum Tum
    Tum
When I Left Burnley for
    Saddleworth
When the Lovebird Leaves its Nest
When the Sun says Goodbye to the
    Mountains
With Someone Like You
White Wings
Ye Banks and Braes
Yes We have No Bananas
You are my Sunshine

NOTES

1. Both quotations are transcribed from my own field recordings which hereafter are indicated by '(T)'.

2. 'The Shepherds Meet: Calendar Carousel', directed by Nick Gray, Yorkshire Television, networked on ITV, 4 November 1982 and 1 July 1983.

3. See Carl von Sydow, *Selected Papers on Folklore*, edited by L. Bødker (Copenhagen: Rosenkilde and Bagger, 1948), pp. 13-15, on the 'Bearers of Tradition'.

4. See *Reminiscences of Horsham being Recollections of Henry Burstow, the Celebrated Bellringer and Songsinger* (Horsham, 1911), reprinted edition with a Foreword by A.E. Green and Tony Wales (Pennsylvania: Norwood, 1975), pp. 114-19.

5. James Ross, 'Folk Song and Social Environment: A Study of the Repertoire of Nan MacKinnon of Vatersay', *Scottish Studies*, 5 (1961), 18-39 (p. 19).

6. Dennis Ellam, *Daily Mail*, 2 December 1981, p. 16.

7. The date of this 'Look North' feature is not known, but it was shown twice during the Summer and Autumn of 1981.

8. The two rooms were made into one and joined to the bar by two archways during 'modernisation' in Spring 1985.

9. A version of this song recorded at the Stanhope Arms, 17 November 1972, and featuring Arthur Howard and others can be heard on *'A Fine Hunting Day': Songs of the Holme Valley Beagles* (12 inch L.P. LEE 4056, Leader, 1975).

10. See my essay, 'Parody and Performance' to be published in a volume of the Open University Press 'Popular Music in Britain' Series, due out in 1987.

11. See *A Fine Hunting Day*, liner notes, pp. 1-12.

12. A transcription is published in 'The Christmas Goose', *English Dance and Song*, 43, no.4 (1981), 7.

13. An analysis of 'The Egg' is included in Russell, 'Parody and Performance'.

14. See note 9 above.

15. Bob Copper, *A Song for Every Season: A Hundred Years of a Sussex Farming Family* (London: Heinemann, 1971), and Frank Kidson, *Traditional Tunes: A Collection of Ballad Airs* (London: Taphouse, 1891), reprinted edition (Wakefield: S.R. Publishers, 1970).

16. Both songs can be heard on Arthur Howard, *Merry Mountain Child* (12 inch L.P. HD006, Hill and Dale, 1981), privately produced record, available from Bridge House, Unstone, Sheffield S18 5AF.

17. See note 3 above.

18. *A Singer and her Songs: Almeda Riddle's Book of Ballads*, edited by Roger D. Abrahams (Baton Rouge: Louisiana State University Press, 1970), p. 154.

AN ETHNOMUSICOLOGICAL APPROACH TO
TRADITIONAL MUSIC IN EAST SUFFOLK*

Carole A. Pegg

In discussing humanly organised sound in *How Musical is Man?*
(Blacking 1973, 5) John Blacking proposes that divisions between music
and ethnic music or art music and folk music are arbitrary and
ethnocentric. He suggests that there is a consensus of opinion in all
societies about the principles on which the sounds of music should be
organised and that the most important distinction, therefore, is between
music and non-music. However, my research in East Anglia showed
that not only do musicians and listeners distinguish between different
forms of music, choosing the ones they prefer to participate in, they also
draw different parameters between music and noise or non-music.
Opinions differed, for instance, within the village of Blaxhall. Geoff
Ling, a local traditional singer, said in reply to my comment, 'It's nice to
hear you sing', 'They call it making a noise, don't they, the young 'uns
do'.[1] Mr Shaw, on the other hand, a former bellringer, considered it to
be the young ones who make the noise. He remembered how, one New
Year after the Ship had shut, the company had set off for the church to
ring the bells. They only got half-way—to the crossroads by the parish
room—when a spontaneous 'tune-up' began, with Fred Pearce on
melodeon and Eli Durrant stepping in the road. 'They don't have music
like they did', he sighed, 'used to have a story to it. Now it's all
noise.'[2]
   One night after a session at the Golden Key in Snape, a group of folk
musicians came back to my house for coffee. I put on a television
programme called 'The Old Grey Whistle Test'. Included in the
programme was an extract from a 1976 film of Jimmy Hendrix
accompanying himself singing the song 'Wild Thing' on electric guitar.

*This paper was given at the 'Traditional Song' conference at Leeds, 20
November 1982, and accompanied by the video film, *Tune-up at the Ship*,
directed and produced by Carole Pegg, 17 July 1982.

Hendrix pioneered the use of feed-back and wah-wah,[3] techniques which are commonplace among electric bands today. His music is characterised by soaring imaginative leaps rooted in a strong melodic sense. Moreover, although he was an exponent of the psychodelic music of the 1960s, the influence which Robert Johnson and Muddy Waters had had on his adolescence ensured that a healthy blues foundation underpinned his music. Hendrix is acknowledged amongst rock critics today as being 'the most important instrumentalist in the history of rock music' for the way in which he extended the boundaries of that form of music (Logan and Wooffinden, 1982, 107-108). One of my visitors, a man in his late twenties called St John, who is himself a blues-influenced guitarist, became very agitated: 'That's not music—that's noise' he protested, adding 'He can't play the guitar. He's distorting the sound so much you can't tell if he's playing it right or not.' The assembled company vociferously agreed.[4]

The Peacocks are retired middle-class incomers to Blaxhall and tenants of Grove Farm. Through one of their children they have become personally acquainted with Pink Floyd, a psychodelic rock band who first came to the fore in the 1960s. They have experimented with sound, incorporating weird electronic noises—as well as more mundane ones such as the ringing of an alarm clock—into their music (Pink Floyd, 1973). Knowing that Pink Floyd were tax-exiles in Switzerland for a while, the Peacocks conceded that they must be successful. The music they produce, however, is so alien to the Peacocks *as music* that they concluded that the band's enormous following must be based abroad rather than in England.

One final example will suffice. On 10 July 1981 a flower festival was held in the local church. Local people contributed. The choir sang and later played the handbells. Two small children played violins helped by their local teacher on viola. Two teenage girls played flute and clarinet. Smiles abounded until a black gospel choir from Bentwaters (an American base only five miles away) made their contribution aided by an electric guitar. As the harsh glorious sound filled the church the congregation shifted uncomfortably and the choir grimaced. Clearly then, even within a small village such as Blaxhall, one person's music is another person's noise.

Blacking further suggests that it is unimportant whether a person listens to country-and-western, pop or classical music. He is more concerned with the structural relationships between music and social life (Blacking 1973, 32). I propose, however, that the *differences* in musical taste can be all important in reaching an understanding of such relationships. Why do some people choose one sort of music to play or listen to rather than another? What has influenced their choice? Why can we not all understand each other's music? Is there a connection between choices people make in music and how they fit into the structure of society? It was with questions such as these in mind that I set out to examine various musical communities in and around the village of Blaxhall, East Suffolk.

Before proceeding further I should perhaps give a brief outline of the development of the parameters of ethnomusicology as a discipline. The publication of Alan Merriam's book *The Anthropology of Music* in 1964 was a significant landmark since it systematically set out a badly needed method and technique for the subject. Prior to the publication of this book there had been much debate about the scope of ethnomusicology. Bruno Nettl in 1956 suggested that ethnomusicology should be 'the science that deals with the music of peoples outside of Western civilisation'. In 1959 Jaap Kunst, on the other hand, saw it as encompassing all peoples 'from the so-called primitive peoples to the civilised nations' but wanted it only to include the 'traditional' music and musical instruments of all cultural strata of mankind. He suggested including 'all tribal and folk music and every kind of non-Western Art music'. Gilbert Chase in his article 'A dialetical approach to music history' (Chase 1958, 1-9) brought the time element into it. He distinguished between ethnomusicology and musicology. Ethnomusicology, he said, should concern itself only with 'the musical study of *contemporary* man to whatever society he may belong, whether primitive or complex, Eastern or Western'. The past, he considered, should be left to 'musicologists'. Charles Seeger, however, disagreed. He felt that ethnomusicology and musicology should not be separate disciplines but part of the same discipline (Seeger 1961, 80).

Following Seeger, Merriam suggested that ethnomusicology should be a fusion of the musicological and the anthropological. His definition of ethnomusicology was 'the study of music in culture'. This should include the technical aspects of musical analysis, that is, an examination of the structure of the sounds produced and taxographical details of the instruments producing those sounds. But it should also consider the behaviour which produced those sounds. Music, then, should be investigated not as an aesthetic object in itself but should be seen in

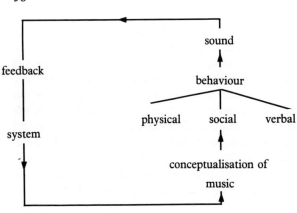

Figure 1. Merriam's theoretical research model for ethnomusicological study.

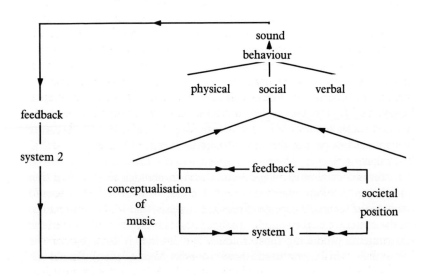

Figure 2. An augmentation of Merriam's model.

relation to both its performance and societal context.

Merriam's theoretical research model has three analytic levels. (See Figure 1) Ethnomusicological study must start at the bottom, he says, for this is what shapes behaviour. To get at this, data must be collected on the distinction between music and noise, sources of musical ability, and so forth. An analytical evaluation can then be made based on an understanding of the 'folk evaluation'. This is the ideational aspect of human organisation, and does not itself produce music. The social aspect of human organisation, that is, behaviour is required for this and Merriam divides this second analytical level into physical, social and verbal behaviour. The third analytical level is the material aspect of human organisation, the product of sound. This has a structure and may be a system but cannot exist independently of human beings. Its structure and presentation is shaped by both conceptualisation and behaviour. The last step in the model concerns the learning theory of human organisation. Listeners accept or reject the sounds they hear as proper or improper in their culture and therefore there is a feedback system from the product to the conceptualisation level. Musical sound is then the end result of a dynamic process. It is ever-changing because of the learning process. Musicians adjust performance to the criterion of the culture and new behaviour changes the form of the sound.

The model is interesting. My chief criticism of it is its holistic approach to culture. As I illustrated at the beginning of this paper conceptualisation about music, that is beliefs about the boundary between music and non-music, differ according to the informant's age and position in society. Even within one small village there was wide disagreement as to what constituted 'music'. Information is needed, then, at the base of the model to take account of this. Account must also be taken of the fact that, whilst a person's position in terms of sex, age set, and social stratum affects conceptualisation or 'sound-ideals', it is by no means a one way process. The model should then look something like Figure 2.[5]

It seems then that there has been a parallel development within the disciplines of ethnomusicology and folksong studies. The internal structure of songs is no longer the prime objective of folksong collectors as it was in the nineteenth century. Interest has broadened to the person who sings the song, the 'bearer and shaper of this cultural tradition'. Ethnomusicology incorporates musicology or the technical aspects of musical analysis but has similarly broadened to include the anthropolo-

Geoff and Nora Ling, Fred 'Pip' Whiting (bones), and 'Font' Whatling during a tune-up at the Ship, Blaxhall.

Photo by C.A. Pegg

gical, that is, how the individual fits into his or her society. In order to understand this it is necessary to live in the area under study and anthropologists usually do this for a minimum of one year. (Participant observation is an important fieldwork technique.) All societies have their own forms of music. Our complex hierarchical society has many differing forms of music. Let us return to look historically at Blaxhall.

Social Structure in Blaxhall during the late Nineteenth and early Twentieth Century

Blaxhall village is isolated, lying in the middle of the old Sandlands, the coastal strip of light sandy soil much of which remained heathland until the closures of the eighteenth and nineteenth centuries. White's *Directory of Suffolk 1853* describes it as

> .... a straggling village, SSW of Saxmunden, NE of Woodbridge, 577 souls, 1975 acres of land. Partly in the manor of Valence, property of Mrs Sophia North and J.G. Sheppard.

The village was divided then. It was partly in the manor of Valence and partly in the manor of Ash Biggotts. From the early eighteenth century until 1923, the Ash Biggotts manor was owned by the North family of Glemham Hall, situated about three miles from Blaxhall. The manor of Valence was owned by the Sheppard family of Campsea Ashe High House until early this century.

Throughout the nineteenth and early years of this century there was, as Newby has pointed out, a rigid hierarchical social structure in Suffolk (Newby 1977, 27). Jean Robin describes the Essex village of Elmdon in 1861 in class and occupational terms as a pyramid, the apex of which was formed by the gentry and the base by the farm workers (Robin 1980, 1-18). Blaxhall could be similarly described. The class structure was marked by a great disparity of wealth. The labouring men in Suffolk were, in the latter half of the nineteenth century, the poorest in England, living on well below the national minimum wage. Agricultural labourers needed to poach game in order to supplement their diet. In 1845 the issue of the Game Laws were raised in the House of Commons and East Suffolk was singled out as an example. Bright, who was calling for an inquiry, linked the intense poaching activity with the terrible conditions in the area, saying that many lived in 'sheds or barns' and that 'they seemed in fact to lead almost a savage life' (*The Bury and*

Norwich Post and East Anglian). The situation was not much improved at the beginning of this century. Robert Savage was earning eleven shillings a week as a shepherd in Blaxhall in 1903 (Dunn 1980, 39). This was less than the Suffolk average wage which was in any case less than the national average (Bowley 1900).

Those at the opposite end of the social structure had no such problems. Weekend parties were held in the big houses in the area throughout the nineteenth century and well into this century. Colossal breakfasts were indulged in before the departure of a fleet of cars to where the beats took place. During one afternoon in 1915, three guns shot over 1,000 pheasants (Clark 1963). After a busy day's shooting the company would settle down in the evening for some quiet entertainment. The agricultural labourers would, on the other hand, gather at the local pub for a 'tune-up'.[6] A consideration of the music engaged in by people at the extremes of the social structure will be helpful.

The Music of the 'Dark Village'

The agricultural labourers might be thought of as forming their own 'musical community', with its own rules. The music played in 'tune-ups' was a mixture of traditional music and popular music of the day. It was performed in public primarily by men. The womenfolk were allowed into the pub but they would sit separately in the kitchen. 'Tune-ups' were controlled by a 'chairman' and in the Ship, until the late 1950, this was Alf 'Wicketts' Richardson. The chairman would keep, 'lovely order' aided by his cribbage board and call upon each person there to contribute. 'Sing, Say or Pay' was the rule. Those who did not sing would play a tune on the melodeon, fiddle, mouthorgan, concertina, or hammer-dulcimer and those who could do none of these things would have to stand the whole company a round of beer. Traditional singer Percy Ling recalled:

> Years ago you got one crowd in Blaxhall—the Smiths, the Lings and the Leeks ... About 7.30 George Ling used to start with a chorus and then we'd start round. Sing a song or pay for a gallon. (Summers 1977-78)

'Outsiders' or 'strangers' were not welcome in these 'tune-ups'. But, as Frankenberg pointed out in his study of Glynceiriog in Denbighshire on the border of Wales, to be a stranger in the sense of an outsider does not necessitate being from outside of or new to the area (Frankenberg 1957).

Tune-up at the Ship: Oscar Woods (melodeon) with gypsy Kenza Diaper stepdancing. *Photo by C.A. Pegg*

None of the farmers from the seven farms in the parish of Blaxhall were welcome, neither were their servants or the gamekeeper. Residence was not the criterion and neither was class, for most agricultural labourers from neighbouring villages would also be unwelcome. Cyril Poacher, singer and cowman at Grove's Farm, Blaxhall, for thirty years reminisced about the time when men from different villages would steer clear of one another:

> There was a time when Blaxhall and Tunstall couldn't agree nor us and Snape very sharply—and they hated the sight of Blaxhall chaps at Little Glemham . . . you didn't used to go round different pubs much, except during the war years, when the beer was rationed and they'd run out at the Ship. (Summers 1977-78)

And the late George Ling described how the blood used to fly in the Ship:

> Cor, there was some blood flying I'll tell you. . . if ever a stranger came in the pub—oh dear, all eyes would be on him. (Summers 1977-78)

There has been more blood spilled in the Ship, it is said, than pints sunk.

Musicians, however, seem to have been exceptions to this rule. In the 1920s, for instance, fiddler Fred 'Eely' Whent would come over from Wickham Market with old Arthur Baldry who also played fiddle and Spanker Austin on 'cello. Sometimes they'd be joined by Reuben Kerridge, a mandolin-banjo player from Snape and often they would find hospitality with the gypsies, spending the night in the caravan of 'Lightenin' Jack' and Fred Smith. Arensberg and Kimball pointed out that lack of 'reciprocity' was a criterion of 'strangership'. They told, for instance, of a man who had been resident in Luogh in County Clare for fifty years. He did not reciprocate in the borrowing of mowing machinery or the lending of boys to each other and was therefore still considered a stranger (Arensberg and Kimball 1968). In Blaxhall visiting musicians reciprocated actively in 'tune-ups'. Not only did they contribute tunes but they accompanied others who stepdanced. The status of 'stranger' was therefore not applied to them.

Most people present in a 'tune-up' in the Ship were interrelated. Their roles overlapped in kinship, work, and play. The 'Sing, Say or Pay' custom already described indicates that the contribution of song, tune, rhyme, or dance was more important than any errors made during that contribution. Since all contributed there was no division between audience and performer. Each in turn was both. Hobsbawm and Rudé suggest that a village might be seen as a dual community, that there was a communal solidarity to which the employers, whether farmers or landlords, did not belong. They refer to this as 'the dark village' as opposed to the "official village" which included landowners farmers, clergy, and professional people (Hobsbawm and Rudé 1969, 62). Only members of the latter were recorded in the new County Directories. It seems likely that the reciprocal exchange of music and song had a consolidatory function for these agricultural labourers at the base of the hierarchical social structure, the members of the 'dark' or 'unofficial' village.

The music made by these people was influenced by their social and economic position. An examination of the instruments played will illustrate this. The single row, four stop, four voice melodeon was the instrument most favoured by English traditional country musicians after the turn of the century. By the term melodeon (or melodion) I mean a diatonic instrument with double action, a button keyboard for the right or melody hand, and simple double action bass chord keys or buttons for the left hand. This contrasts with the single action chromatic accordion with its button or piano style keyborad for the right or melody hand, and its more complex arrangement of bass chord buttons for the left hand. A melodeon has always cost roughly one quarter the price of an accordion and the single row, four stop, four voice is the cheapest available melodeon. It could—and surprisingly still can—be acquired for the cost of a week's wages (Hobgoblin 1980, 2). Oscar Woods, the current melodeon player at the Ship, pointed out that whilst melodeons were considered reasonable for adult workers—for a boy it was more difficult. In 1930, for instance, when a double row melodeon could be bought for £3 this would still make it difficult for a boy:

> Cause a boy what worked in a farmhouse as back'us boy used to get about 9/- or 9/6d a week, din't 'e. If he got ten bob that would be recognised as pretty good, y'see.[7]

Charlie Whiting from Southolt, a melodeon player until he lost two fingers in an accident, told how he bought a melodeon on hire purchase at six pence a month in 1919 when he was fourteen years old:

> I got in a hell of a muddle over the payments—it was a rum job to keep up. (Summers 1977-78, 35)

As it was a cheaper instrument to buy, many boys began on the mouthorgan and only later graduated to the melodeon. Fred Pearce, for instance, melodeon player at the Ship, began playing the mouthorgan at six years and did not start to play the melodeon until he was twenty-four. Similarly Fred List played mouthorgan at school and only later played melodeon (Summers 1977-78, 35).

Concertinas were more expensive to buy than melodeons and consequently were less popular. There are two main types of concertina— the English concertina which can achieve a smooth scale by using alternate hands for each succeeding note of the scale and the Anglo-German concertina which has the same double-action as the melodeon. The London concertina-making firm Crabb and Company have stock sheets which show that between 1889 and 1895 three 30-key Anglos were being made each week with a retail price of £3.55. By comparison 48 key English concertinas were being produced by Lachenal for £17 and by Wheatstone for about £25. The English concertinas were popular in the Victorian drawing rooms of the middle classes and Anglos were used by traditional English country musicians (Digby 1978).

Hammer-dulcimers too were expensive to buy. Norfolk hammer-dulcimer player Billy Bennington relates how, when his father was young around 1890, the cost of a dulcimer from a professional maker in Norwich called Withers was £5. As Billy pointed out 'That was a lot then'.[8] The dulcimer was, however, an instrument which it was possible to make at home. Jimmy Cooper, the Glaswegian dulcimer player explained that not only were shop instruments too expensive, they were not as good as home-made ones. They were not built strongly enough and were therefore not loud enough. They were also not made with seasoned wood as thy should be (Kettlewell 1976).

I have a large dulcimer which was made by William Lawrence of Comberton in Cambridgeshire. As a young man in the early years of this century Lawrence would work as a builder's labourer during the winter months of each year. But with the arrival of the summer he would put his dulcimer on his back, hop onto his bicycle along with his cousin Herbert Thriplow (who also played the dulcimer), and tour the village feasts. They would sometimes be gone for weeks at a time. If he failed to pay his way Lawrence would then sell his instrument at the end of the summer and make a new one during the following winter. He would use an old cupboard or table for the body and the staples from sheep hurdles for pegs.[9]

However, economics was not the only variable affecting choice. An important consideration was style. Until the early years of this century the most popular instruments for accompanying dancing in country areas were the fiddle, hammer-dulcimer, and pipe and tabor. As I have described elsewhere (Pegg 1983), country fiddlers had a distinctive style which combined a choppy bowing technique, an aggressive tone, with no use of vibrato, and double-stopping and drone notes thus providing a driving rhythmic sound suitable for dancing. Musicians had to adapt their playing techniques to make the hammer-dulcimer rhythmic since the natural 'after-sound' or ringing on of the strings countered this. This 'after-sound' did, however, have the affect of a drone which was integral to the fiddle style described above and an element of the 'sound-ideal' which country musicians chose to perpetuate.

The western free-reed 'Mundharmonika' or 'mouth-organ' was invented by Friedrich Buschmann in Berlin in 1822. Hand-operated bellows to propel air through the free reeds were then added and this was marketed in 1829 under the name 'Akkordion' (Dallas 1979). At the turn of the century melodeons and accordions were being imported into Britain at the rate of 25,000 per annum. But other instruments had been available to country musicians before. Why should they suddenly decide to adopt these particular instruments for the purpose of continuing the tradition? The preference of traditional musicians for double-action instruments was significant. Since the bellows must alter direction for each consecutive note of the scale, it was impossible to produce a smooth sound. The instruments had, then, an in-built rhythm. Moreover, the tone produced was strident and powerful and drone notes were readily available. The necessary elements of style intrinsic to the 'sound-ideal' of these musicians were, then, contained within the instruments themselves.

I am not suggesting that these were the only variables affecting choice. The function of the instruments was primarily to accompany step-dancing in East Suffolk and this necessarily affected style. Similarly musicians often had to walk or bicycle several miles to the place of performance and therefore portability was a factor to be considered. All of these things would combine to influence the agricultural labourers' conceptualisation of music or 'sound-ideal' which would then, as I have suggested in my augmentation of Merriam's model, affect musical behaviour and the sounds produced. A brief look at the music engaged in by those at the opposite end of the social structure will help to illustrate my point.

The Music of the Upper Classes

In the big houses on the outskirts of the village the landowners were enjoying a different kind of music. This was part of a European musical tradition. An examination of the North family records brought to light a bundle of manuscript and printed music, some of which was presented in manuscript form by composers to members of the North family in the eighteenth and nineteenth centuries. The collection included an Aria in three-part harmony, selections from operas such as 'Sixteen pieces from the celebrated Opera of Il Flauto Magico, composed by Mozart, adapted for the Piano Forte or Harp and with an accompaniment for the Flute'; selections from ballets such as

Il Convitato di Pietra
Grand Ballet
by Mr Le Picq
as performed with great applause at the
KING'S THEATRE 1785
the music by the celebrated
Chevalier Gluck
in which he introduced a favourite
PAS DE TROIS

which had been adapted for harpsichord, pianoforte, violin and flute; dances from operas such as 'The Favourite Opera Dances 1787 performed at the King's Theatre Haymarket and adapted for Pianoforte, Flute or Violin'; music for trios of two violins and bass, duets for two violoncellos or two violins and solos for flute, violoncello or bassoon. Other instruments catered for were the harpsichord, the 'English Gittar' (Cittern) and the 'Italian Pocket Guittar'. Also in the collection were some scale exercises for the piano, a treatise on Principles of the Science of Tuning Instruments with Fixed Tones and advice on transposition (North Family Records).

Two separate traditions of music existed simultaneously then within one small geographical area. The music of those at the base of the triangular social structure was local in that it was kinship-based. The music reflected the fact that the labourers' universe was bounded by the market town, the fair, and an area of perhaps fifteen or twenty miles distant (Hobsbawm 1969, 57). Individuals owned songs and tunes and they thus became extensions of their own personalities. Tunes were often named after their owners such as 'Charlie's Waltz' (which hammer-dulcimer player Reg Reeder inherited from his grandfather Charlie Philpott) or 'Earnie Seaman's Polka' (which melodeon player Oscar Woods inherited from his hero Earnie Seaman). Songs were often localised by the insertion of familiar place names. Both songs and tunes were inherited according to principles of ownership within families and between friends. The music was primarily oral, non-literate, and operated according to social rather than aesthetic rules. There were few instruments and these were either cheap or home-made and portable. Choice was influenced by social, economic, and historical factors.

Those at the apex of the triangular social structure, on the other hand, operated within a universe in which the county was the smallest unit. The music they chose to engage in reflected their greater mobility. Musicians were often patronised and brought in from outside the area for weekend parties and the music performed was from an international repertoire. It was a literate form of music, based on western European musical rules and operated according to different social rules. Since there was a marked division between audience and performer, aesthetics were important. Instruments were expensive, often non-portable, and bought rather than made at home.

Over the last thirty years the composition of the village of Blaxhall has altered dramatically. Mechanisation in the 1950s contributed to this. Less men were required on the farms and many young men left looking for jobs elsewhere. Members of the middle classes began buying property in the country. The Campsea Ashe and Glemham Hall Estates have been gradually selling off farms. The High House at Campsea Ashe no longer exists. The Cobbold family reside at Glemham Hall and have opened the house to the public. In the absence of the big houses the classical music tradition has found an alternative abode at the Snape Maltings, only one and a half miles from Blaxhall. Once providing employment for up to one hundred men it now houses the prestigious Aldeburgh Festival. The programme of the 34th Aldeburgh Festival in June 1981 covered much the same spectrum as the collection of music already described from Glemham Hall. There was some opera, some chamber music, string quartets, and choral singing, music for trios and for unaccompanied instruments. The instruments played were the same as those played at the weekend parties at the big houses—violin, guitar, bass, 'cello, flute, piano, and harpsichord.

For this paper I have chosen to look diachronically at Blaxhall and the surrounding area and have attempted to show how people's conceptualisation of music and their 'sound-ideal' and subsequent decisions about music-making were not arrived at in a vacuum but influenced by variables such as social and economic circumstances. Because of limitations of space I have dealt only with those social groups at the top and bottom of the hierarchical social structure. My work includes those groups in-between: the artisans and tenant farmers. I am also undertaking a synchronic analysis of the area which, because of the proliferation of the middle classes, the expansion of education, and the growth of the mass media is necessarily more complex (see Pegg 1983, 1984 and 1985).

NOTES

1. Geoff Ling, the Blaxhall Ship, 30 November 1980.
2. Frank Shaw, his home in Blaxhall, 25 August 1981.
3. 'Feed-back' occurs when not only the sound of an instrument is received through its microphone pick-up but also the sound from the instrument's amplifier. Having gone through the system once the sound is fed back into the pick-up for a second time. 'Wah-wah' is achieved by manipulating a floor unit by the foot. This unit contains a treble and a bass booster. If the foot is rocked back and forth (forward for treble, backwards for bass) it can make an instrument sound as if it is talking or crying.
4. 21 February 1981, Holly Cottage, Blaxhall.
5. A more detailed outline of the development of the discipline of ethnomusicology is to be found in Pegg 1981, 60-74.
6. 'Tune-up' is a local expression for a musical session. See *Tune-up at the Ship*, a video film directed by C. Pegg, 17 July 1982.
7. Video film interview with Oscar Woods and Carole Pegg at the Ship, 17 July 1982.
8. Personal interview with Billy Bennington, Rose Cottage, Barford, Norfolk, 13 November 1980.
9. Dr Russell Wortley told me this story and it was Russell's widow Diane who kindly gave me William Lawrence's dulcimer.

References

Arensberg, C.M. and Kimball, S.T.
  1968   *Family and Community in Ireland*, Cambridge, Mass.: Harvard
          University Press
Blacking, J.
  1973   *How Musical is Man?*, London: Faber and Faber
Bowley, A.L.
  1900   *Wages in the United Kingdom in the Nineteenth Century*, Cambridge:
          Cambridge University Press
The Bury and Norwich Post and East Anglian
  1845   Wednesday 5 March
Chase, G.
  1958   A Dialectical Approach to Music History, *Ethnomusicology* 2,
          pp. 1-9
Clark, K.
  1963   The Other Side of the Alde, *Tribute to Benjamin Britten*, London:
          Faber and Faber
Dallas, K.
  1979   The Beginnings of the Folk Industry, *Folk News*
Digby, R.
  1978   150 Years of Crabb Concertinas, *Folk News*
Dunn, G.
  1980   *The Fellowship of Song: Popular Singing Traditions in East Suffolk*,
          London: Croom Helm
Frankenberg, R.
  1957   *Village on the Border*, London
Hobgoblin Catalogue
  1980   1 August
Hobsbawm E.J. and Rudé, G.
  1969   *Captain Swing*, London: Lawrence and Wishart
Kettlewell, D.
  1976   The Dulcimer, Unpublished Ph.D. Thesis, Loughborough:
          University of Technology
Kunst, J.
  1959   *Ethnomusicology*, The Hague: Martinus Nijhuff, Third Edition
Logan, N. and Wooffinden, B.
  1982   *The Illustrated Encyclopedia of Rock*, London: Salamander Books
Merriam, A.P.
  1964   *The Anthropology of Music*, Northwestern University Press
Nettl, B.
  1956   *Music in Primitive Culture*, Cambridge, Mass.: Harvard University
          Press

Newby, H.
  1977   *The Deferential Worker*, Harmondsworth: Penguin Education
Pegg, C.A.
  1981   Review Article: Ethnomusicology—A New Branch of Anthropology,
            Cambridge Anthropology, 6, no. 3
  1983   Musical Choices and Traditional Suffolk Musicians, *Cambridge
            Anthropology*, 8, no. 1
  1984   Factors Affecting the Musical Choices of Audiences in East
            Suffolk, England, *Popular Music, A Yearbook*, ed. R. Middleton,
            Cambridge: Cambridge University Press
  1985   Music and Society in East Suffolk. Unpublished Ph.D. thesis.
            Department of Social Anthropology, University of Cambridge
Robin, J.
  1980   *Elmdon, Continuity and Change in a North-West Essex Village
            1861-1964*, Cambridge: Cambridge University Press
Seeger, C.
  1961   Semantic, Logical and Political Considerations Bearing upon
            Research in Ethnomusicology, *Ethnomusicology* 5, pp. 77-80
Summers, K.
  1977-78   Sing, Say or Pay, *Traditional Music*, Nos. 8 and 9

                            Discography

Pink Floyd
  1973   *The Dark Side of the Moon*, Harvest Records

SONG AND SOCIAL CONTEXT*

Michael Pickering

The notion of attempting to understand a particular text or set of texts in relation to a social and historical context is nowadays a reasonably well-established principle in the methodology of folksong scholarship. Some of the best work in the field, from A.L. Lloyd onwards, is marked by this commitment to developing a social and historical understanding of popular and traditional song and music. Yet there has been little discussion of why contextualisation is important or of what it involves. What I want to do in this paper is to outline the rudiments of a contextual approach to the study of locally performed popular song.[1] I want to tackle the question of what we mean by context and what it means to contextualise any cultural item or artefact. I should stress that what I'm offering is only a tentative sketch, a provisional statement, and all I hope to achieve here is to suggest some of the values of a contextual approach—as I conceive it—and perhaps to set off a few hares as well. My outline is oriented primarily to the study of locally popular song in the rural England of the nineteenth century, though I hope that what I have to say will have relevance to other periods and places as well.[2]

No song exists in isolation, in a social or cultural vacuum. As text and performed event, a locally performed popular song always bears relations with other songs in an evolving repertoire, and with a multi-faceted and likewise evolving social culture which people encounter and experience and contribute to. Song exists as and within a cultural process, and those who live this process have never been merely bearers or carriers of song texts and tunes: they have only been seen in that way across a class divide, viewed by folksong collectors as though they were, so to say, servants with sealed messages from the past delivered on a

*This is a revised version of the paper given at the 'Traditional Song' conference at Leeds, 20 November 1982.

musical platter to a master or mistress. The message or meanings of songs are never immutably sealed, but shift and vary according to a range of social variables characterising particular performers and audiences (gender, for example, or socio-economic status) and according to the historical and cultural contexts, occasions, and social settings, in which they are conceived, and received, as the performance weaves the weft of words and tune in time together across the warp of situated consciousness. So what I think we should first recognise is any song's context in a whole repertoire, or repertoires, associated with both individual and groups, which leads secondly to seeing its context in a particular song and singing tradition. Expanding the focus from this, we need next to distinguish between specific, yet at the same time connected, micro-social contexts involved in song transmission. These one may categorise as contexts of production, performance or reproduction, reception, dissemination, and recording or collection.[3] Because the complex relations between these specific contexts are variable they can only be appreciated when studied in place and period, and with respect to the ways such relations are shaped and steeped within a developing social structure and historical process.

This is to begin to identify the different types of context to which we should attend. What connects them in the process of a song's assimilation into social practice is the ideology and shared consciousness of people situated in particular cultures. Within the matrix of their culture and shared consciousness, singers and audiences are, in greater or lesser degree, active participants in the realisation of textual and musical meanings, and in the realisation of the significance of those meanings for a local, and to a different extent, wider popular culture. In considering these crucial features of song transmission, we should eschew any unproblematic relationship between text and social context, between what a song comes to signify and the structure of social relations in a particular setting and environment. Cultural texts do not relate in any transparent way to a social context. Song, as an artistic product and activity, cannot be understood simply in its own terms, or viewed as an autonomous realm of creative work isolated from its contexts of production and consumption. But song as well cannot be understood as if it stood in direct correspondence to specific social and historical conditions. Song texts do not simply reflect or mirror a society or specific class interests, material conditions, or forces of production. While they are inextricably bound up with social contexts and relations, with ideology and consciousness, it is important not to lose sight of the specificity of song texts and tunes—their particular aesthetic texture and value—and important as well to see song as always in some sense a mediation and construction of social reality. I shall return to this point later.

The issue I want to deal with first is this involvement of people themselves in negotiating the relations between text and context. The social history of popular song (whether ephemeral or traditional) can profitably devote itself to the study of popular music's external features, such as performance styles or singing occasions, but it has also to address itself to such questions as the relationship of song texts to popular attitudes and mentalities. These kinds of question involve the problem of meaning. In approaching this problem we need first of all to recognise the genesis of a song's meanings as rooted in the text itself. This may seem an obvious point, but it is important to make in order to guard against voluntarist conceptions of the assimilation of song, and against the notion of a limitless number of possible readings which can be made of a song. The linguistic, literary, and musical content of a song, the ways it is structured as a vocal and melodic composition, constitute the basic pattern and frame of any interpretation and understanding. What a song means at any time is, to varying degrees, conditioned by the poetic text: the text delimits and initially generates the possible number and type of meanings which can be derived from it. But song meanings are not simply immanent in a text, something deposited there and awaiting extraction. The corollary of this is that signification and value are not static, definitive, or universal. Song texts are polysemic or polysemantic. They contain different orders of meaning or potential meaning which may be differentially realised, re-created, and evaluated. The meanings encoded in a text at the moment of its production are not necessarily the meanings made and understood by its various recipients. Certain meanings—certain invited readings— may of course be privileged and preferred in the text itself, but there is no guarantee that such meanings will be preferred by either performer or audience.

Texts become modified and tunes changed in the process of transmission across time and place, but so also do their meanings and significance. Re-creation of meanings and their re-evaluation occur in particular contexts, and are always conditioned by various contextual processes and features. At one level, these range from the skill and style of performance to the composition of audiences and the contexts of particular singing occasions. But at another level the realisation of a song's meanings, and the consequences of those meanings for both individual and group, are also profoundly influenced by the social and cultural world people inhabit in the present, and by their relationship to the inherited, congealed experience of the past. The ways in which various individuals and groups involved in song performance and transmission understand and appreciate song texts and tunes is inevitably related to their personal and social identities. If we cannot understand locally performed popular songs historically outside of the group and community contexts to which they were in some sense felt to belong, then in investigating those groups and communities we need to look at such factors as their members' linguistic and cultural competence, educational background and opportunities, folkloric repertory and resources, common sense and morality, and their social position in terms of status, role obligations, expectations, power, independence, and self-orientation.[4] It is important to take such factors into consideration, where we can, precisely because performers and audiences make songs have certain meanings ideologically and socially. As I said earlier, a song does not simply release a pre-ordained meaning (or meanings) when voices give it utterance, and it is in order to gain some sense of the situated meanings of song texts realised by particular groups and communities that we need to explore the social and historical contexts in which that cultural process occurred (or occurs).

In the kind of contextual approach I am outlining, emphasis should be not so much on the texts of songs and ballads and what these tell us of their historical contexts, or vice versa, but upon the contextual mediations of these texts. The relationship of singers and audiences to song texts within mental and material contexts always involves a dialectic between limiting conditions and creativity, between structure and agency. One aspect of this, which I regard as crucial to any consideration of the popular assimilation of song, is the process of discovering or creating cultural proximity. What I mean by this is the situated process of assimilation of an element or practice into a given cultural or subcultural formation, the creative process whereby meaning is accommodated to people's ideology and place in society. This occurs both in relation to innovation within the present, and to the modification of traditional elements according to the changed social relations of the present. While men and women are, in the context of their own social experience and lives, to varying degrees active participants in the creation of a sense of the relatedness and significance of cultural products, whether externally derived, inherited, or indigenous to place and period, this process is also to varying degrees structured and conditioned by given circumstances and contending ideological forces and by the nature of people's own presence in their own history and culture. Accordingly, the extent to which the realisation of cultural proximity and value is active and integrated, or relatively broken down, can perhaps serve as a rough measure of the vitality or decrepitude of any specific local culture.

'Context' is a loose, vague, and elastic term, yet it is a keyword in the study of culture and one which it seems, for lack of anything better, we're unavoidably stuck with. Because of this, we need to be more precise in our conception of particular contexts—and of their inter-relationships—in time and place. While these need to be studied empirically in relation to particular song texts and repertoires, and particular musical practices and traditions, I think it would be helpful to make a conceptual distinction between situational and structural contexts. Such contexts may be distinguished for analytical purposes but in historical terms they must be seen as co-existing, embedded as it were within each other. The immediate contexts of song production, performance, reception, dissemination, and collection are all situational. As such they are specific to particular moments of the cultural process of popular song transmission and distribution, and each have varying constituent features and dimensions. These situational variations of context are themselves located within, and conditioned by, a historically contingent structural context, characterised and defined by particular modes of production and consumption, and by their social organisation and relations. The social contexts of performance or collection have therefore to be understood in relation to the particular social order in which those contexts of performance or collection occur. When we are concerned to contextualise at the level of the structural, we are concerned with questions of social organisation and change, and, at least within a capitalist social formation, with questions of class division and class legitimation. Yet such questions must themselves be understood not only in relation to the broader context of the social structure, but also in relation to the specific and concrete contexts in which people interact.

We need the notion of structural context because song performance occurs in and through social relationships which are structurally conditioned. We need the notion of situational context because song performance also occurs in immediate and particular situations which focus and articulate combinations of general structural factors and contradictions in ways which are often specific to local traditions, communities, and social groups. The two notions are complementary in that they refer to distinct but interrelated dimensions of the relationship between social structure and general social interaction. The understandings which local singers and audiences have of songs and ballads are influenced both by their position in the social class structure, as experienced in local milieux, and by the way they ideologically negotiate social encounters and the social contradictions and ruptures they experience as a group or class. The dynamics of song texts and song performances in specific situational contexts cannot therefore be divorced from the broader structural context in which social division in an unequal and exploitative social order is manifested, legitimated, and at times contested.[5]

English village song, culture, and tradition in the nineteenth century, while never static, homogeneous, or existing in splendid isolation, nevertheless constituted the main indigenous influence and resource available to village labourers and artisans in their attempts to make sense of their lives, their place in a patriarchal and class society. In other words, popular culture and tradition (in which I include religion), as manifest in its various situational contexts, was for many members of the rural working class virtually the only major stock or reserve upon which they drew in negotiating the broader context of a class structure and patriarchal order which in many ways shaped their own way of life—or way of oppression. We need therefore, in the cultural analysis of locally popular song, not only to situate song within particular milieux and group-oriented cultural configurations, but also to understand those milieux and configurations in their relationship to the social structure. The nineteenth century village singing occasion, for example, occurred in a range of situational contexts, but these contexts were in certain ways defined and placed by a wider context of social structure and organisation, so that now the general village concert, the smoking concert, quête customs involving song, club suppers, workshop singing, church and chapel music, taproom performances, harvest-home sing-songs and so on have all to be seen and assessed contextually, in relation both to the defining characteristics of particular situations involving song performance, and to the structural determinants of those particular situations.

While my discussion of popular song and popular musical practice is oriented to its study in a particular local community, following from my research for *Village Song and Culture*, I do not see a contextual approach as limited to localised studies.[6] Its benefits can be realised in other kinds of study, and I will give just a few examples of these. It can for instance be applied to the study of song relating to specific occupational cultures, on a more regional basis, or to the biographical study of a particular songmaker and singer, where that study is concerned to use an individual's life pattern as the focus of a wider examination of the social and cultural contexts in which it evolved.[7] It strikes me as well that a historical study of nineteenth century women singers is crying out for someone—preferably a woman—to do. Indeed, we need at least several such studies, looking at songs sung by women in particular geographical contexts, and relating these songs to the historical context of women's position within the family, within sexual relations, within labour, and within social life generally.

It will perhaps be evident by now that what I understand by a contextual approach to locally performed popular song implies a broader cultural and social analysis than is involved in the new concentration on communicative processes, rather than texts or genres, advocated by those American folklorists slightingly dubbed by Richard Dorson as 'young Turks'.[8] This loose grouping of scholars tend to counterpose ethnographic, performance-oriented studies of folkloric transmission against the undoubted limitations of a textually monopolised approach. What I am suggesting is a need to include ethnographic and interactionist accounts in an altogether more comprehensive analysis. In moving towards this, we need firstly to see how song performance and reception relate to the characteristic features of a particular way of living and looking at the world. We need to relate song to other elements within particular cultures and to show how the various elements of these cultures change and conflict as well as being traditional or normative. Secondly, we need to situate that kind of account in broader patterns of social and cultural change. It is important to stress the historical dimension in the social analysis of particular cultures, for at any one time the complexity of the sociological features of a community react with and are reacted upon by the complexity of historical forces. Within cultural traditions, for example, the accretions and sedimentations of past formations always have a particular existence in the present, and insofar as those traditions do not cast a moribund shadow over the living, their content resounds within the context of present needs and situations. From this kind of approach, then, a sense of continuities, divergences, and specifities will be gained, so that we become aware of what characterises a particular community culture and what distinguishes it from others in space and time. Any cultural item or element can then be tackled in relation to this overall appreciation of its social and cultural location and specificity as well as in relation to those artefacts and expressive forms shared with other cultural and subcultural formations across and within time. It is not only a question of taking into account the interrelations of elements between particular cultures over space and time which matters though, for these diverse forms of interaction are of course inseparable from political forces and pressures deriving from the structural organisation of a social order, and bound up with either the maintenance and naturalisation of that order or with efforts to challenge and subvert it. It is then precisely in this context that we should be critical of the intrusion of romantic generalisation and the ideological notions of eternal verities and common applicabilities which, among other things, have marred the study of so-called folksong for far too long. Indeed, the notion of folksong itself must be understood historically as an ideological construct originated and perpetuated outside of the cultural contexts of popular musical traditions and practice, a facet of the wider and complex effort of a dominant bourgeois culture to win and exert control over the nature and composition of popular culture and popular cultural activity—to remake the popular in its own image.

Once we have accepted the general proposition of the inseparability of text and context, and acknowledged the problematic nature of the term context, we must then proceed to ask: do we work back from a text or texts into a conceptually schematized context, or do we primarily study the historical record and analytically weave the texts or texts into that record? Alternatively, do we instead tack dialectically between the two approaches? My own inclination is to go for the latter option. Song texts do not tend to provide objective knowledge of historical reality, yet they do generally relate, albeit obliquely, to that reality as lived. The aesthetic experience of song is of necessity interpretative, and the interpretative processes involved in experiencing song within a historically contingent ensemble of intersecting situational and structural contexts inevitably occur, at least in particular communities, within the mould of a shared cultural world and of the wider social experience more or less common to those for whom a song acquires communal as well as individual value. This is not to reduce the aesthetic nature and experience of song to the social and contextual. Clearly, the specific constituents of song need to be identified and discussed, and in a general sense this will mean seeing the aesthetic process of song transmission as involving a symbolic transformation of the natural and social reality—or realities—to which it relates, and within which it is produced and reproduced. This production and reproduction of song are socially and ideologically located, mediated, and constructed, yet cannot be dissolved into social and ideological processes. We need therefore to develop a dialectical approach to studying the formal specificities and features of popular song, and the situational and structural contexts of its transmission. In developing such an approach, our understanding of a song text will be modified by our knowledge of the social and cultural contexts of its transmission within specific milieux. Our understanding of the processes of cultural assimilation of song, and the construction of meanings in the situated reception of song, will likewise be modified by studying such processes in relation to the initial generation of aesthetic meanings by specific song texts and forms.

One kind of traditional song study which relates to the kind of approach I am outlining is the attempt to examine the historicity of particular song texts. Richard Dorson has spoken of the necessity of the folklorist engaging with history in order to explore 'the historical validity of oral tradition'.[9] Some valuable studies have been conducted along these lines, valuable primarily because they go on from examining the relationship between song texts and the historical record (or account) and revealing the historical nature of particular texts, to investigating the moral, symbolic, and ideological role of those texts within particular social and historical contexts. I am thinking particularly of A.E. Green's study of the ballad 'McCaffery' and David Buchan's study of 'The Ballad of Red Harlaw'.[10] But looking at the cultural relationship between, on the one hand, the selective historical content of a text and the way a text mediates an event or events in the past, and on the other, the range of existing, alternative historical evidence about that event or events, involves only one—albeit crucial—aspect of the text-context dialectic. Study of the historicity of texts is one which should supplement the broader project of attempting to understand the social relations and material conditions of all aspects of musical and popular cultural activity in particular historical contexts.

In studying the song culture of particular people in the past, inasmuch as this is or can be accurately documented, we must be concerned not only with attempts to reconstruct the various occasions in which it played a part and the local culture in which it had an integral place, but also (and much more hazardously) with attempts to understand the ways in which it gave a specific character and colouring to the lives of those people. Our knowledge of *their* history will therefore be enhanced by the effort to understand the social and cultural roles and meanings of particular song texts as embedded in, and nourished by, the humus of their social and cultural contexts. Naturally, imaginative reconstruction, however disciplined, cannot faithfully reproduce the actual experience of past cultural participation and understanding. But in attempting to grope towards approximations of such participation and understanding, popular songs of the past (and past popular cultural content and form more broadly, including folklore) represent an historical source whose value is only now beginning to be appreciated. The same applies to the difficulties involved in any analytical work involving historical popular song. This raises crucial and complex issues of methodology—issues which would require another paper and which it would be frivolous to address simply in passing. The point I wish to emphasise here involves a more initial and general recognition. This is that popular song of the past represents a culturally constructed, coded account which, along with other aspects of the culture of which it was a part, patterned understanding of everyday social and personal life for ordinary people existing in similar circumstances. Aesthetically song involved a cultural transformation of selective features of the empirical world in which such people led their daily existence, and aesthetically it fed into the composite, unsystematic and contradictory understanding of their lives and the society in which they lived. In order to see how and why this was so we need many more studies of song within particular localities and community cultures (so avoiding the sociologically loose and generalised category of the folk), studies of popular song as part of the whole social and symbolic universe inhabited by people within those local milieux. And precisely because of the aesthetically transformative powers and properties of song, we need to be aware of the empirical, contextual realities upon which it drew and upon which it impinged. Only then can we gain some sense of the cultural and ideological roles of popular song within particular ways of life and living, roles which may well have been complemented or in certain ways contradicted by other texts or practices in a local culture.

It is here that we encounter those tricky problems of historical cultural analysis: problems of function and effect. Once again, however we approach these probems theoretically, what are of paramount importance are the contextual factors governing the social and cultural roles of popular song, for there are in the abstract a vast array of such roles, ranging from the stimulation of pleasure and emotion to the communication of critical social comment. The role or roles performed by particular songs depend both upon song content and form, and upon the situational and structural contexts in which and in relation to which particular songs have reference and meanings. The possible social and ideological roles of songs have therefore to be considered within the empirical study of those contexts. It is all too easy either to select examples that fit a particular prescriptive model, or to construct historical fictions on the flimsiest of evidence: Lloyd's claim for the 'Cutty Wren' (uncritically echoed by others) is notorious in this regard.[11] But one thing I think Lloyd's overall enterprise has succeeded in establishing is that while folksong is a product of social and historical process, it can involve as well attempts to make significant responses to objective realities, and at its best, attempts to transcend given historical conditions which in some way constrain freedom: freedom of consciousness and action, and freedom to change existing social institutions and relations. Art may outlast particular historical conditions and contexts because of a recognition and appreciation of this creative effort towards freedom, towards a better life, aesthetically realised.

> In the folk songs of any period, behind the recitals of lost love and violent death, of hanged robbers and sweethearts pressed to sea, of the beauty of a country spring and the hardness of country labour, of transported poachers and colliers on strike, something more is to be heard: the longing for a better life.

As Lloyd goes on to explain, this longing is generally expressed 'by transposing the world on to an imaginative plane', tincturing it with fantasy, transforming bitter and brutal material and social conditions of existence into something beautiful and tragic, 'so that when singer and listeners return to reality at the end of the song, the environment is not changed but they are better fitted to grapple with it'.[12] That describes one important (but by no means exclusive) function of traditional song. It hints also at the complex problem of traditionality. This problem requires separate treatment, but I would just like to make one point here. The aesthetic value of much traditional song in time past and time present is, following Lloyd, lodged in admiration for its imaginative vision and content. To take just one instance: admiration of songs of tradition may be said to occur because the ways in which they were involved in attempts to make significant responses to past contexts, can be compared and contrasted with our own endeavours to make sense of our age and our own lives. Such endeavours necessarily mediate our appreciation of those songs. We admire and enjoy songs of the past not because we are the same as those who sang and listened to them,'but because we are in many ways quite different, because we exist in definite historical relations. Added to the text-context dialectic is therefore a past-present dialectic, and it is vital to take this analytically into consideration.

While acknowledging the immense difficulties this raises, I want to return to the relationship of the textual and the contextual within period and place. I said earlier that we need to oscillate between the study of texts and the study of particular social contexts, understanding such contexts as constituting a complex pattern evolving and shifting over time and irradiating outwards from any particular locus or situation. So, for instance, knowledge of the macro-social context of particular cultures must always inform an ideological analysis of a song text, for while the study of a text in isolation from existing social relations, organisation and action may suggest a narrowly defined ideological effect of that text, knowledge of social context may well work to complicate the issue. In a recent brief study of 'The Farmer's Boy', I have tried to suggest how, in relation to a particular historical context and to its frequent performance in a known village community, the song may have had contradictory or alternative meanings, creating to some degree a manifest ideological effect yet having at the same time an oppositional role—possibly more latent—in that the song could serve as a vehicle for expressing village labourers' aspirations and grievances, and perhaps also working as an affirmation of village community values in relation to customs of hospitality and mutual aid, and the question of fair reward: values increasingly denied by capitalist farmers within the characteristic rural social relations of the Victorian period.[13] These different levels of possible meaning understood in context may perhaps suggest something of the nature of the social consciousness of those for whom the song had a real resonance and force, a mode of consciousness caught thus in a brittle thread of light and revealing briefly its resourceful yet incoherent complexity.

The kind of approach I have sketched is to be distinguished from that which is encountered in some social history and which, however diffidently, uses literature—in the widest sense of the term—as decoration or illustration unproblematically embellishing a narrative presentation. It is to be distinguished as well from an approach which one finds in some conventional literary criticism, which fills in a few token details of the historical background and then goes on to privilege a study of the text, often universalising its textual meanings in the process. I am not suggesting a dismissal of the skills and tools of literary or textual criticism in the study of historical popular song. Critical means for appreciating poetic imagery, symbolic meaning, narrative structure, tone and style are clearly valuable. Attention to song content and structure obviously has to remain a vital component of folk and popular song methodology (structuralism and semiotics is proving increasingly useful in this regard) but that attention should complement a broader cultural and historical analysis rather than, as too often, displacing it.

In taking a historically contextual approach to the study of song and music, we have to be aware of and take into account the ideological mediations of those people responsible for recording popular song and music in the past. In other words, we have to be aware of the social relations characterising the contexts of collection. The studies of Sharp and Child by Dave Harker, and Vic Gammon's study of folksong collecting in Sussex and Surrey, have been valuable examinations of the difficult historical resource which folksong collections represent.[14] That kind of source criticism is vitally necessary to a contextual and relational approach. Having made that kind of examination, though, the analysis of popular song texts as manifested in their social contexts involves an investigation of the characteristic aspects of the particular socio-economic and political conditions and structures which impinge upon cultural processes at any time.[15] The heuristic value of this is that it should help avoid seeing and interpreting those processes only and wholly in terms of either the informant's, the collector's, or the academic's individual perception and cognition of a set of texts and of the ways they are mediated by their micro- and macro-social contexts. In the end, the underlying purpose of a contextual approach, as far as I am concerned, is to gain some sense of what popular song in past time actually meant in ordinary culture, how for instance it coloured and textured social, political, familial, and sexual relations at a particular time in history. In short, the quest should be to discover the ways in which popular culture was, and is, actively made and assimilated by producers, performers, and their publics.

In bidding farewell to the antiquarian fetishism of curious objects and cultural oddities, the emphasis in the study of folklore and popular culture should therefore be on cultural and historical process, on people creatively making what they can out of what for the most part they inherit and are given. The folklorist and the student of popular culture necessarily work within an interdisciplinary field, and have therefore to learn and draw from those areas of enquiry and analysis which overlap with their own. Social history is an obvious example. As Benjamin Botkin put it years ago:

> What the historian must bear in mind above all in determining what is and what is not folklore is the fact that it is the history and not the origin of a given place of lore . . . that makes it folklore. Thus 'Oh Susanna' originally written by Stephen Foster as a pseudo-Negro song, became a typically American folk song only when it became the theme song of the forty-niner. Just why and how this particular song appealed to the miner in his particular socio-economic situation concerns the social historian as well as the folklorist. In this sort of thing folklore and social history are inextricably bound up with each other, and are not simply common ground but one and the same ground.[16]

One could make similar (though guarded) points about certain aspects of social anthropology, sociology, and social theory, cultural studies, semiotics, sociolinguistics, and ethnomusicology.

Song is a social relation. It is socially produced and consumed. What the example from Botkin suggests is that songs have both use values and exchange values. That is, they have a value in use in that they may satisfy some emotional need, or express what people have only felt and not articulated for themselves, or contribute to a person's understanding of the social world he or she inhabits. Popular songs also have exchange value: they can be exchanged for something else, which is a value quite opposite to their use value. When we speak of cultural commodities we are referring to the unification of these opposite values: the commodity is a form which unites them, but in a contradictory relation. Where songs are produced and sold as a marketed artefact, their exchange value is predominant but not exclusive; their use or aesthetic value may also be realised within or shortly after an exchange transaction. Conversely, where songs have entered into individual and communal repertoires, their use or aesthetic value prevails. Such value, however, can never wholly escape a market origin (no matter how much song texts become subsequently modified in transmission) in that such a context of production inevitably constrains the artistic creation of song texts by tailoring them to maximise their commercial potential (a potential which is, of course, at the same time variably affected by consumer taste and demand). It is now firmly established that the majority of the folksongs we find in the major Victorian and Edwardian collections were originally printed by broadside entrepreneurs and distributed within a commercial nexus.[17] It is vital to take such factors into consideration. Yet we must also take into consideration the fact that many broadside songs and ballads attained only ephemeral popularity.[18] Where songs entered into tradition (or traditions) we need to explore why particular groups or communities assimilated and valued them, how their exchange value became metamorphosed into their aspect as use value.[19] The transmission of songs from their contexts of production to contexts of consumption involves an integration of exchange value and use value, and if folksong possesses any residual worth as a cultural term, it is in its suggestion of the endurance of a contextual use and aesthetic value in song beyond an original exchange value, an enduring value realised and reinforced in a subsequent process of transmission (whether oral or not) occurring via repeated performances over time. Why this is so for particular songs within particular communities can, I am claiming, only be understood through empirical study of the contexts in which it occurred or occurs.

Locally performed popular song must therefore be related to the culture of which it is or becomes a part, to a culture inherited as tradition yet at the same time evolving as tradition within any period, to the connections between that culture and other patterns of culture, and to the overall structure of social organisation within particular historical periods. The ethnography of song performance is then but one dimension within a combination of contextual processes and structures. The discipline of contextualisation involves identifying who is involved in what and on what basis at any one time and in any one place, and certainly with regard to the study of the popular music of the past it involves, *inter alia*, getting behind what the earlier collectors said (and ignored) about songs, singers, and audiences. It is not, however, only a question of debunking bourgeois ideology; the analysis of folk music by people like Lloyd, Marothy, or Kodaly, or Adorno's critique of twentieth century popular music, need also to be critically evaluated. It is as important to ask whether Ewan MacColl may be praised as it is to ask that question about Cecil Sharp. Contextualisation also involves us being aware of the dangers of taking particular notions and concepts peculiar to—and a product of—our own historical period, and utilising these uncritically in the analysis of past cultures and past cultural forms, idioms and content. It is not only the insensitive usage of sociological and anthropological typological categories or analytic constructs which are a risk. We must also be reflexive about the keywords of our own scholarly domain: 'tradition' and 'traditional', 'culture', 'community', 'popular' and so on, for these can also get in the way of understanding the contextual experience of song and music.[20]

I suggested earlier that no socio-cultural analysis of popular song should fail to be sensitive to its specificities as an artistic product and activity, yet my discussion has been skewed in the direction of song texts. Song is of course a complex vocal and musical process, and the relationship of words to tune or melody must accordingly be explored. How do they interrelate and mutually combine? This raises a further problem, for though words and music mutually affect each other within the dynamics of performance and reception, they are not similarly structured as communicative forms governed by given cultural codes and conventions. While musicological and ethnomusicological analysis is capable of distinguishing the generic characteristics of—and relationships between—different types of musical structure, such approaches do not to my knowledge provide adequate means for analysing musical aesthetics and meaning.[21] Whether the lack of a developed semantics of music is due to academic shortcomings or to the relative weakness, capriciousness, or diffuseness of musical signification is an issue on which I reserve my judgement. Having said that, and having acknowledged the importance of identifying and comparing different musical conventions and idioms within (and between) cultures, I would continue to stress the relatively greater importance of investigating the social relations and contexts of popular musical activity. Social relations and contexts unavoidably affect and to a high degree characterise musical styles, events, delivery and reception. And the meanings accorded to such aspects of musical practice are socially and ideologically determined in an analogous way to the meanings accorded to particular song texts and their familiar tunes. In other words, music is as much a field of articulation of class distinction as any other area of artistic production and practice, and cannot therefore, in a class society, be divorced from the politics of culture, from ideological struggle. But while cultural competence is unequally distributed and ultimately contributes to the legitimation of class division, people can nevertheless use what resources and aptitudes they have at their command in participating in that struggle. Working class kids may not be into opera, but there are some who can't dig punk.

Moving towards a conclusion then, we can say that while the way individuals and groups respond to song texts is influenced by their class position within particular social and historical contexts, so the way in which they respond to the ensemble of social relations and contexts through which and in which their everyday lives are moulded is at the same time influenced by the cultural products and processes at their disposal, and by their ability to appropriate and assimilate that which is available to them. This whole question must also be seen in relation to the historically determined scope which people have for modifying or more fundamentally changing their world, and in relation to social and cultural change occurring outside of their immediate or even long-term control. Both endogenous and exogenous change have an effect on the way in which people come to respond to the content of particular song and singing traditions, and popular cultural content, forms, and institutions more broadly. Whether a song, body of songs, or a particular musical genre continues as an active part of any tradition depends on the extent of intervening socio-economic (and sometimes technological) changes, and on concomitant transformations in the beliefs, values, attitudes, assumptions, precepts, and general moral framework of a social collectivity. It is for this reason that there is always some sort of correspondence between a song's longevity in tradition, and change in its meanings and value made in response to broader patterns of social process and change. Returning to an earlier point: the performance of particular songs or types of song may well be because of their difference to contemporary social life. They may well be revered precisely because of their pastness, their identification with the past, and their discrepancies with the present. The importance of contextualisation here is self-evident.

I have in this paper both ignored and glossed some crucially important issues (for example, questions of method), and offered a very condensed treatment of other complex problems. In defence I can only claim that my purpose has been to be suggestive, and to sketch only certain aspects of a contextual approach to the study of locally performed popular song. Lack of time inhibits anything more thorough. I have as well, in outlining an approach to the study of popular song among small groups and in local community contexts, presented a somewhat ideal version of what should be involved: for various reasons, it may not be possible to be as comprehensive in establishing contextual characteristics and interrelations as I have suggested is desirable. Again, lack of time inhibits anything more thorough. Empirical research difficulties require a paper in themselves. But in finishing, I would say that for me at least, the necessity to develop a contextual and relativistic approach arises firstly out of the usual response I have when reading collections like the two volume set of *Later English Broadside Ballads*, or Peter Kennedy's doorstopper of a book, *Folksongs of Britain and Ireland*: my mind after a while goes into a sort of giddy blur of historical understanding;[22] and secondly, from the recognition that the production and reproduction of artistic forms among social groups is subject to a dense web of mediating contexts, processes, and influences, and in the study of such forms, all these complex articulations have in my view to be taken into account. It seems to me, in short, that only through employing the discipline of context can we really hope to challenge, and replace, those approaches to the popular music of the past which deny its place within a whole ensemble of meanings, practices, contexts, and institutions, and which deny its contribution to the ways in which past generations lived their own existence.

NOTES

1. While I reject the terms 'folk' and 'traditional' as applied to situated song performance and prefer here the term 'popular' as more properly relating to the *whole* musical activity of the people, I retain the analytical distinction between local (or small group) and more extensive popular cultural transmission. It is essentially with the former process that this paper is concerned. The emphasis is therefore on the communication of song within specific group or community contexts. While such communication generally exhibits a distinctive mode and manner, the whole point of the paper is to suggest that local communicative and aesthetic processes cannot be studied socially and historically in isolation from the wider contexts of cultural production and social order. It is precisely in relation to these broader strata that the semantic and conceptual difficulties associated with the term 'popular' become manifest. See, for instance, S. Hall,

'Notes on deconstructing the "popular"', in *People's History and Socialist Theory,* edited by Raphael Samuel (London, Boston and Henley: Routledge and Kegan Paul, 1981), pp. 227-40.

2. This particular orientation derives from the popular music research in which to date I have been most engaged.

3. The transmission of song can begin in any one of these contexts: they are neither hierarchically nor serially ranked. They are also, of course, not of necessity indispensable for each other.

4. One of the most progressive and challenging socio-cultural schemes for approaching the study of folkloric and popular cultural conceptions of the world is Antonio Gramsci's. See *Selections from the Prison Notebooks* (London: Lawrence and Wishart, 1978); and for two useful recent guides, see the section on Class, Culture and Hegemony in *Culture, Ideology and Social Process*, edited by T. Bennett and others (London: Batsford, 1981), pp. 185-260, and *Approaches to Gramsci*, edited by Anne Showstack Sassoon (London: Writers and Readers Publishing Cooperative, 1982), particularly the article by A.M. Cirese, 'Gramsci's Observations on Folklore', pp. 212-47.

5. While I agree with Dan Ben-Amos that the small group is the defining locus of folklore performance as popular artistic communication, both folklore and small groups are structured by wider social and historical forces than the dynamics of aesthetic practice and small group interaction, and both folklore and small groups have therefore to be understood not only within the situational and group contexts which characterise folklore peformance, but also in terms of hegemonic structure and class power relations. See Dan Ben-Amos 'Towards a Definition of Folklore in Context', in *Toward New Perspectives in Folklore*, edited by Américo Parades and Richard Bauman (Austin and London: American Folklore Society, University of Texas Press, 1972), pp. 3-15.

6. See Michael Pickering, *Village Song and Culture* (London and Canberra: Croom Helm, 1982).

7. For examples of the kinds of study referred to, see Roger Elbourne, *Music and Tradition in Early Industrial Lancashire 1780-1840*, The Folklore Society Mistletoe series (Cambridge: D.A. Brewer, and Totowa, N.J.: Rowman and Littlefield, 1980); *The Rambling Soldier*, edited by Roy Palmer (Harmondsworth: Penguin, 1977); *A Singer and her Songs*, edited by Roger D. Abrahams (Baton Rouge: Louisiana State University Press, 1970); Edward D. Ives, *Larry Gorman, the Man who made the Songs* (Bloomington: Indiana University Press, 1964); Edward D. Ives, Joe Scott, *The Woodsman-Songmaker* (Urbana, Chicago, London: University of Illinois Press, 1978). (This list is, of course, in no way exhaustive.)

8. *Folklore and Folklife*, edited by Richard M. Dorson (Chicago and London: University of Chicago Press, 1972), p. 45. The 'Young Turks' specifically identified by Dorson were Roger D. Abrahams, Dan Ben-Amos, Alan Dundes, R. Georges and Kenneth Goldstein. (A debate over text-context relations,

involving such scholars as D.K. Wilgus, S. Jones, Ben-Amos, R. Georges, and Y. Zan, has been conducted in American folklore journals over the last ten years or so. Comment on this debate would need detailed treatment elsewhere.)

9. Dorson, *Folklore and Folklife*, p. 7.

10. A.E. Green, 'McCaffery: A Study in the Variations and Function of a Ballad', *Lore and Language*, 1, no. 3 (August 1970), 4-9; no. 4 (January 1971), 3-12; and no. 5 (July 1971), 5-11; and David Buchan, 'History and Harlow', *Journal of the Folklore Institute*, 5 (1968), 58-67 reprinted in *Ballad Studies*, edited by Emily B. Lyle, Folklore Society Mistletoe series (Cambridge: D.A. Brewer, and Totowa, N.J.: Rowman and Littlefield, 1976), pp. 29-40. See also A.L. Lloyd, 'On an Unpublished Irish Ballad' in *Rebels and their Causes: Essays in Honour of A.L. Morton*, edited by M. Cornforth (London: Lawrence and Wishart, 1978), pp. 177-207.

11. A.L. Lloyd, *Folk Song in England* (London: Faber, 1967), p. 100, and *The Singing Englishman* (London: Workers' Music Association, 1951), pp. 7-9, 30. See also Reginald Nettel, *Sing a Song of England: A Social History of Traditional Song* (London: Phoenix, 1954), p. 52; S. Finkelstein, *How Music Expresses Ideas* (New York: International Publishers, 1976), p. 23; and S. Sedley's, comment, *Red Letters*, no. 14 (Winter 1982-83), 2. An examination of Lloyd's claim is made in Pickering (1982), pp. 74-76.

12. A.L. Lloyd, *Folk Song in England*, pp. 183-84. See also A. Silbermann, *The Sociology of Music* (London: R.K.P. 1963), p. 197: 'For the musical experience is . . . not only a flight from social struggles, but at the same time an embodiment of those struggles. It is useless to baulk at this paradox; for if there were no dialectic, no ambiguity in music, then the musical experience would reach just that stage of uniformity and vulgarity so often predicted by misanthropic observers of culture, but which, from the very nature of the musical experience itself, cannot come about.'

13. Michael Pickering, 'The Farmworker and "The Farmer's Boy"' *Lore and Language*, 3, no. 9 (July 1983), 44-64.

14. David Harker, 'Cecil Sharp in Somerset: Some Conclusions', *Folk Music Journal*, 2 (1972), 220-40; 'May Cecil Sharp be Praised?', *History Workshop*, 14(1982), 44-; and 'Francis James Child and the "Ballad Consensus"', *Folk Music Journal*, 4 (1981), 146-64; Vic Gammon, 'Folk Song Collecting in Sussex and Surrey 1843-1914', *History Workshop*, 10 (1980), 61-89.

15. This kind of investigation is not of course excluded from the work of the two aforementioned authors. See for instance Dave Harker, *One for the Money: Politics and Popular Song* (London: Hutchinson, 1980); Vic Gammon, '"Babylonian Performances": the Rise and Suppression of Popular Church Music, 1660-1870' in *Popular Culture and Class Conflict, 1590-1914*, edited by Eileen and Stephen Yeo (Sussex: Harvester, 1981), pp. 62-88, and 'Song, Sex and Society in England, 1600-1850', *Folk Music Journal*, 4 (1982), 208-45.

16. Bernard A. Botkin, 'Folklore as a neglected source of social history', in

The Cultural Approach to History, edited by C. Ware (New York: Columbia University Press, 1940), p. 314.

17. See Robert S. Thomson, 'The Development of the Broadside Ballad Trade and its Influence upon the Transmission of English Folksongs' (unpublished Ph.D. thesis, University of Cambridge, 1974). As Thomson puts it, folksong collectors of the late nineteenth and early twentieth centuries 'unwittingly experienced greatest success in those districts that had been best served by the broadside-ballad trade' (p. 268). It should be noted that the main purpose of Thomson's thesis appears to be, in some ways quite rightly, to contest the romantic and nationalist associations which adhere so strongly to the term folksong, rather than to explore the relationship between the commercial origins of the majority of collected folksongs and their enduring popular appeal.

18. Thomson estimates that only about 15% of broadside output has been perpetuated in folksong tradition (p. 24).

19. Gramsci makes the point that even though the majority of popular songs are written 'neither by nor for the people', people selectively take over such songs according to their own criteria and because they conform to their own 'way of thinking and feeling'; such songs become representative of popular conceptions of 'life and the world, in contrast with official society'. See A.M. Cirese, p. 226.

20. For a useful introductory guide to such terms, see R. Williams, *Keywords* (London: Fontana, 1976).

21. See, however, L.B. Meyer, *Emotion and Meaning in Music* (Chicago and London: University of Chicago Press, 1956), for a psychologically oriented study of musical 'meaning', and the theoretical studies by Susanne Langer, *Philosophy in a New Key* (Cambridge, Mass.: Harvard University Press, 1978 edition), chapter 8, and Malcolm Budd, *Music and the Emotions: The Philosophical Theories* (London: Routledge and Kegan Paul, 1986). The problem is of course also tackled in various ways in the more sociological work of scholars like Weber, Adorno, Finkelstein, Henze, Shepherd, Etzkorn, Kneif, Blaukopf, and Silbermann. This point about the inadequacy of the analysis of the language of music is, however, made in relation to music *qua* music.

22. *Later English Broadside Ballads* edited by John Holloway and Joan Black (London: Routledge and Kegan Paul, 1975), and *Later Broadside Ballads*, Volume II (London: Routledge and Kegan Paul, 1979); *Folksongs of Britain and Ireland*, edited by Peter Kennedy (London: Routledge and Kegan Paul, 1975).

SONG MANUSCRIPTS AND
THE ACQUISITION OF SONG REPERTOIRES
IN ORKNEY AND SHETLAND*

Alan Bruford

The use of manuscripts by traditional singers, apparently as aids to memory, is something which most folksong collectors in English-speaking areas will have encountered. This paper is intended to illustrate this use from the writer's experience in the Northern Isles of Scotland (Orkney and Shetland) and ask tentatively two questions: what influence the manuscripts have had on the formation of individual singers' repertoires, and whether they are meant as aids to memory or something else?

First the scene must be set. The Northern Isles had entirely lost their variant of the Norse tongue (Norn), apart from a few archaic rhymes and spells, by 1800 in favour of a strongly accented Scots retaining some Norse words and one or two grammatical features. Their older traditional songs, with a couple of exceptions, range like those of mainland Scotland from the stilted English of broadsides to broad Scots which sometimes includes local words but is more often the artificial Anglo-Scots dialect of classic ballad (Henderson 1983). Very few of these can be said to be native to the islands: the so-called 'King Orfeo' (Child 19, Shuldham-Shaw 1976), only collected in the North Isles of Shetland but possibly related to a Middle English poem; 'The Grey Selkie' (Child 113, Bruford 1974), basically in 'ballad Scots'; and the New Year Song, 'St Mary's Men', which has absorbed extraneous

---

*The paper given at the 'Traditional Song' conference at Leeds, 20 November 1982, was largely centred round a selection of tape-recorded songs which were used to illustrate various facets of repertoires. This paper represents an alternative version which might have been given without using sound recordings, and contains the main points made in the original version about the use of manuscripts together with new details of the various singers, their MSS, and the writer's contact with them.

elements including parts of a ballad about Henry II and Fair Rosamund (perhaps because 'St Mary's men' sometimes became 'Queen Mary's men', and Queen Mary had been married to the faithless 'King' Henry Darnley), and, in the only version still regularly sung, the mainland Scots New Year rhyme, 'Get Up Auld Wife and Shak yir Feathers'.

These last two have been collected in both Orkney and Shetland. More recent local compositions, from this century and the last, are seldom known outside a single island or parish; twentieth-century examples may be comic or sentimental songs in local dialect, but these have no basis in older tradition. Songs about shipwrecks, the most frequent genre of local composition earlier, are in broadside English. The broadside repertoire is one that could be found anywhere in Britain, and songs from the south of England ('As I Came Over Salisbury Plain', 'The Bold Ramillies') or Ireland ('Sally Munro', 'The Middlesex Flora') are as common as Scottish ones. One or two, as we shall see, were claimed for Orkney (where it is difficult just to collect 'old songs' because everyone assumes you want 'Orkney songs') and others were localised by adding local place-names: 'Farewell to Stromness' is the song Ord printed as 'The Emigrant's Farewell to Donside' (Ord 1930, 350). 'The Derby Ram' was actually known in Orkney under four different titles—the original, 'The Ram of Durham', 'The Ram of Bervie' from mainland Scotland, and 'The Deerness Ram' from Orkney itself.

There is an earlier stratum of imported song, shared by Orkney and Shetland, in Scots rather than English and long enough established to have some local dialect forms in them. Some of these are short lyrics, often used as dandling songs for children or mouth music for dancing: typical is 'Saw Ye nae my Peggy', alias 'Saw You me Maggie?' (*Tocher*, 2, p. 35) sung in Orkney and Shetland to varying tunes which share a rhythm much simpler than the version given by eighteenth-century Scottish songbooks, and probably closer to the early form of the folksong. Others are classic ballads, and most of the ballads collected in Shetland may belong to this stratum. In Orkney the situation is complicated by the influx of farmers and farmworkers from Aberdeenshire and surrounding counties who came to the bigger farms in the last century, bringing a rich singing tradition with them. So the Orkney song tradition at the beginning of this century was much like that which Greig and Duncan collected, including classic ballads, Scots lyrics, broadside ballads and even bothy ballads. The islands probably had more sea songs than landward Buchan: certainly Greig's Orcadian correspondent T.S. Towers, a Sanday man who was schoolmaster at Tankerness in the East Mainland, was his sole source for some of them. Before 1914 in Orkney, it is clear from many descriptions I have recorded, singing was the regular entertainment at weddings and harvest homes ('muckle suppers') and could often be part of an ordinary evening visit. As in the Victorian drawing-room, everyone had a 'party piece', song, recitation or trick, and many had sizable repertoires, though with the coming of the wireless and the gramophone few people continued to remember the songs they once knew.

In Shetland the situation seems to have been different, at least over the past century. Like several other fieldworkers, I have found it comparatively hard to collect songs there. The most obvious explanation is that the strong and individual fiddle-playing tradition in Shetland took precedence over singing, but this is not entirely satisfactory. For one thing, the fiddle was mainly played for dancing, and there was as much dancing, including reels peculiar to the islands, in Orkney as in Shetland, though instruments such as melodeon and accordion may have challenged the fiddle's pre-eminence sooner in Orkney, and there were evidently a good number of pipers there, so that one hears of pipers leading wedding processions where in Shetland this was the fiddler's place. The absence of the Aberdeenshire immigration in Shetland is certainly another factor, confirmed by the fact that it has been harder to find songs in some of the North Isles of Orkney such as Westray and Rousay where there were fewer incomers. (I have recorded an interesting range of songs from a Rousay man, Malcolm Hourie, only to find he learned most of them working on a farm in the West Mainland, near Stromness.) There is some reason to think that at the beginning of the last century singing, fiddle-playing, and storytelling were all important entertainments throughout the Northern Isles, but where singing became more favoured in Orkney on the Aberdeenshire model, fiddling and even more, storytelling, which is still much easier to collect in Shetland, became the usual entertainments there. There may be one further relevant consideration: whereas both men and women sang in Orkney, most older traditional songs recorded in Shetland have come either from women, from former seamen who learned them at sea, or from men who named their mothers as their main sources. As in most parts of Scotland fiddlers were usually men, though there were exceptions, and it seems possible that in Shetland singing was correspondingly a female prerogative, used to accompany women's activities, such as spinning, and entertain small children, and rather looked down on in mixed or all-male company. It may even have been thought unlucky on the fishing-boats where most Shetland men worked, like whistling: I have certainly not heard it mentioned in the many stories and accounts of the haaf fishing I have recorded, while at least two Orcadian informants have mentioned singing on herring boats.

When I first recorded songs in Orkney I already knew that some Scottish singers compiled manuscript collections, for one of my first tasks after joining the School of Scottish Studies was to index a series of recordings made by Hamish Henderson in Aberdeenshire in 1952, many of them from a retired farmworker called Willie Mathieson. Willie had started writing down the words of songs and recitations he heard, and copying others from borrowed manuscripts and broadsides, as a youth in the farm bothies, and his collection filled three large volumes and contained several hundred songs, besides a few (not only bawdy u⌐ ⌐s) he knew but had not written down. He was not a particularly good singer himself, but he could provide a tune to anything in his books that was not obviously a recitation, though in some cases he seemed to be doing it just to oblige, not recalling what he had heard—he fitted a remarkable number of songs to the 'Villikins and his Dinah' tune. I was not surprised therefore when I visited Mrs Ethel Findlater, already well-known as a singer of traditional songs, and found that she had two or three smaller notebooks of songs which she spread in front of herself and her daughter, Mrs Elsie Johnston, when they sang together for me. In later years, when I recorded Ethel on her own for clarity—though she really preferred to sing with someone else—I found that she knew most of the songs well enough to be able to sing them without the book, though if she had it she would hold it in front of her and turn the pages, even if she did not sing exactly the words she had written. Elsie, on the other hand, needed the words: since her mother's death she has sung songs from her mother's books for visiting fieldworkers, but still only knows by heart one or two she has learned for concert performance.

Ethel's song collection was not in fact a very typical one. She told me later that she learned songs in her youth orally from her mother, a cousin, and neighbours and mainly fixed them in her memory by singing to herself while she was 'milking the kye'; in some cases she might have been given a written copy of a new song or written it down on an odd sheet of paper as soon as possible in case she forgot it. The more organised collection in notebooks seems to have followed her discovery first by the Finnish musicologist Otto Andersson in 1938 (who came looking for her husband and noted ballads from Ethel, who sat and sang on the kitchen table) and then by Peter Kennedy, who recorded her with her husband and daughter in 1955. It was apparently one of her neighbours, however, who suggested to Ethel that she should write out the song texts about 1960, following her husband's death—perhaps as therapy—and it was only after my first visit in 1966 that she sat down to copy her entire repertoire into a single foolscap ledger, an unused account book from her late brother Sandy Harvey's joinery business (see Figure 1). Into this went not only the songs in the other notebooks, but texts she had from newspaper cuttings and many from her head, learned both from local singers and from the modern media—records, radio and latterly television—so that they ranged from 'Binnorie' and 'Lord Lovel' to 'The Isle of Capri by Val Doonican'—and a country-and-western favourite of hers in 1967, 'The Blackboard of my Heart' ('My tears have washed "I love you" from the blackboard of my heart') which she thought I should record from her. Ethel knew the difference between what she called the old 'ballad songs' and recent releases, but any song that told or implied a story, preferably a sentimental one, was a good song to her, and the 106 songs in the book give a sample of what was circulating in Orkney over sixty years. The ledger contained not only texts of songs but the notes of their tunes in tonic sol-fa above (or occasionally below) the first verse, though with no indication of rhythm or underlay except the arrangement into four lines corresponding to the first verse, they would be hard to interpret without a recording to help.

One notebook whose contents went into the ledger had not been written by Ethel herself. She had borrowed it from a shepherd's daughter, Violet Harvey, who had left the neighbourhood some fifty years earlier. Violet, now Mrs Manson, twice married and widowed, lived about five miles away in Sandwick, and in preparation for my second visit Ethel cycled over with her songbook to learn the tunes of some of the songs in it she did not remember or had never got. Luckily Violet was able and willing to help. She lent her a second songbook, also written before 1915, and when eventually Ethel introduced me to her she recorded a good range of shorter songs and riddles as well as the ballads in her book. However, I never succeeded in recording her older sister who was reputed to have a notable repertoire. Violet's book,

14.

Oh' daughter dear, dry up your tears,
An dwell no more in sorrow;
For I'll wed ye tae a far higher degree,
Than your plueman boy from Yarrow.

15.

Oh' father ye've got seven sons,
An ye can wed them all tomorrow;
Bit ye'll ne'er wed' me tae a fairer one
Than the one I lost on Yarrow.

16.

This girl she being so deep in love
Wi' her ploughboy lad from Yarrow;
Her tender heart it soon did brake,
And she died through grief an' sorrow.

The Ballad of the Standing Stones. (Stennes Orkney.)
Tune.

m s l l l d r ni ni m r
d r ni d t l r
d r ni l l s m ss m r
d r m r m s l l.

1.

In one of these lone Orkney Isles,
There dwelt a Maiden fair;
Her cheeks were red, and her eyes were blue,
And she had yellow curling hair.

2.

Which caught the eye and then the heart,
Of one who never could be;
A lover of so true a maid,
Or fair a form as she.

Figure 1 Ethel Findlater's Manuscript showing the contents page and page 44. The pages do not begin until page 35 because it was written in the second volume of a pair of ledgers.

written in her teens, if not before she left school at twelve, is more typical of manuscript song collections in Orkney. It contained some long ballads presumably ultimately from broadsides, though they have evidently passed through oral tradition before being written down again: for instance the first song in the book, a version of 'The Gosport Tragedy', where the murdered girl's ghost appears near the end, opened 'In Ghostsport of late. . .', a nice piece of folk etymology.

The typical song notebook in Orkney, then, seems to have been one written mainly when the compiler was young, probably under twenty, and those I have seen were mostly written between the 1900s and the 1930s, though one I borrowed from Miss Helen Tulloch, written by her mother, one of the notable Scott family in North Ronaldsay, could well date from before 1900. It too was written in an account book. Ethel Findlater borrowed two books for me to photocopy from a neighbour, Mrs Work, whose half-sister, Maggie Kirkness, had compiled them not long after the turn of the century: one, which included rough copies of songs in the other, was written on a tiny unlined memo pad just four inches by two-and-a-half. There may have been a competitive element in the making of the books: one substantial collection I borrowed and recorded tunes to was made—again, in an account book—by George Low in the East Mainland between the Wars (see Figure 2), closely following on one that his older brother David had made. David Low left his notebook to his sister, later Mrs Sydney Manson, when he emigrated to Canada as a young man, and I was able to compare the two. Obviously they had often taken down the same songs from the same sources, or copied from each other, but George had added others after his brother went away. George Low, unlike Ethel Findlater, had very definite ideas on what should be included: he felt that songs like 'The Bride's Lament' (Laws K10) and 'The Jams on Gerry's Rocks' (Laws C1) were newcomers to the tradition and barely merited inclusion, though Laws' catalogue gives evidence that both of them date from the 1860s in North America: they may have taken sixty years or more to reach Orkney, and certainly the incongruously cheerful tune known there for 'The Bride's Lament' looks like a music-hall or burlesque treatment. On the other hand the latest young person's collection I have heard of (it was lent or given away and I could not see it), compiled by Meta Wylie, later Mrs Mathieson, as a teenager in Burray after the last War, seems to have been as mixed as Ethel's. Like most of Ethel's big book, it was compiled in bed during a lengthy illness, and obviously opportunities to write out songs were not presented to everyone who might have done so.

Some manuscripts were compiled by singers for their own use: thus the late Mrs Anna Taylor (née Martin) had one of songs which she and her sister Wilhelmina ('Billy') had sung as a teenage duet at local concerts around the time of the First World War. They were largely drawing-room ballads on tragic themes and patriotic favourites from that war or the Boer War like 'Goodbye Dolly Gray', along with three older songs, two nautical ('Canada-i-o' or 'The Wearing of the Blue' (*Tocher*, 38, p. 62), and 'A Lady in her Garden Walking') and one Scots rustic ('Davie and his Kye Together'), learned from a local vanman. Few people would have used their songbooks in this way. Another book, presented to the School of Scottish Studies by Otto Andersson, who was sent it after his visit to Orkney in 1938 by one of the Fotheringhame family from Sanday, was written in 1900 by T.S. Towers, Gavin Greig's correspondent mentioned above. It contained twenty-two songs in beautiful copperplate script, with title-page, song titles, and accurate sol-fa tunes in Gothic lettering, and must have been a gift to a close friend—again, not typical (see Figure 3). The two songbooks I have seen from Shetland are not typical either: they both have sol-fa tunes. One was compiled by Mrs Elizabeth Smith, a teacher like Towers and a writer of dialect songs, and contained some of her own compositions as well as old songs learned from her parents in Bressay and picked up later when she was teaching in Foula and Sandness. The other was made by the notable Fetlar storyteller, Jamesie Laurenson, probably when he was a grown man between the Wars but perhaps when his mother, who seems to have been the main source, was alive. The sol-fa is written over the words so that the underlay, if not the rhythm, is certain, but few of the songs are more than fragments one or two verses long, though some are remnants of 'big' ballads. However, I only succeeded in identifying what Jamesie called 'The Winding Sheet' as Child 155, 'Little Sir Hugh', when his brother Gibbie remembered a line about a well which was not in the book (*Tocher*, 19, p. 92). But the notebook of long, mostly traditional songs, words only, begun in the writer's teens or twenties seems to be the most usual, certainly in Orkney (where I have seen examples from Evie in the Mainland, Stronsay, and North Ronaldsay as well as those mentioned) and probably in mainland Scotland opposite, though I have only recorded one singer who had one, Colin MacDonald, a native of Strath Halladale

Half past ten (36)

(1)
Of mind when I counted my ain life fean
Its oft times I gead, but she seldoms was
For her feathers on Elder, like a goodly men
He age lockid his doors about Half past ten.

(2)
Ea sacrament sunday & sacfranie hame
Ony lad was his lassie wad hae done the same
For we sat and we cracked by the cosy fire end
Till the time slipt awa till near Half past ten.

(3)
The worthy man read, sign is seventhly forage
And when he was done he solemly said
It age been the rule and Its likely ye heny
Slay we look a our doors about Half past ten.

(4)
The hint was enough for a blith lad like me,
But I caught a blith & Jeanies black ex,
As much as to say come you back tae the flen
And yeel maybe stay longer than Half past ten.

(37)

(5)
It right twa three lads and meal did agree
Ta gang awa doon and ta hae a bit spree
Says I what do think but tae gang doon the flon
Well be sure tae be hame afore Half past ten.

(6)
We a were received was a hearty good will,
And the auld man himsel brought a cask of hracil
Sigh gade awa hen, but says from yeel attend
That the doors are a lockid by Half past ten.

(7)
O aye answered fean, but the best o the joke,
Was her slippin ower, and astuping the clock,
And Ill no stop to tell you the why or the when,
But the hands were a pointing tae Half past ten.

(8)
Aboot four in the morning the auld man arrose
And lightin a spurk tae the clock sign he goes
Guid save us quid wife did you hane near near
For the lads are a awa afore Half past ten.

Figure 2 George Low's Manuscript showing pages 36 and 37.
(NB. 'ea' = 'ae', 'sign' = 'syne' 'yeel' = 'ye'll', 'feather' = 'faither'.)

in Sutherland. As I have found only three or four other singers in Caithness and East Sutherland in as many visits— admittedly visits that were mainly directed at collecting oral history or brief digressions on the way to or from Orkney—it seems possible but by no means certain that these areas had less of a singing tradition than Orkney.

There is a rather different tradition of writing song words on sheets which are passed readily from hand to hand; indeed it is common for song-sheets to be written out to give or send to someone interested in a particular text. Thus John Goar, a Sanday man living on the mainland who later became the main traditional singer at the short-lived Orkney Folk Club, composed a number of songs in the traditional vein. Two·of them, about the tragic losses of the fishing boats Ben Doran and George Robb, became quite well known and he sent copies of the words to various parts of the country. He himself had a number of songs, some very roughly written on graph paper, which he had got from neighbours in Sanday, and one of them, 'The Henry Brig', was about a fairly local shipwreck. A song from his own family tradition, 'The Annattee', about a ship wrecked in Sanday perhaps as far back as the eighteenth century, provided the basis for the tune and even the wording of the first verse for the 'The Ben Doran'. Manuscript sheets were particularly used for local compositions: a Mrs Kemp contacted by Ethel Findlater gave me some beautifully written copies of songs written by her father on a local ploughing match and similar subjects, and I have been sent songs by the well-known Orkney song-writer Allie Windwick as well as many more ephemeral compositions. But all sorts of songs could circulate for considerable distances in this form. One remarkable example is a copy of an Aberdeenshire bothy song, 'Drumdelgie', which I was lent by Willie Seatter, a former farm servant and farmer born in Egilsay and an active singer specialising in bothy songs. It was written for him by an 88-year-old former Lothian farm servant he had met in a bar in Edinburgh when he was on holiday in 1966. Eighty years ago a holiday in Edinburgh would have been unlikely for most Orcadians, but girls might have gone there on domestic service, or sailors in the Merchant Navy. Colin MacDonald's mainland repertoire came largely from a great-uncle, who had gone as far as Carlisle as a cattle-drover, and from his father, who as a railway worker for a time also had wide contacts. My colleague Peter Cooke has met several retired merchant seamen in the Shetland Isle of Whalsay with more typical notebooks of traditional song words picked up at sea: most of them of course are sea songs.

A

Collection  of

OLD SONGS,

Selected
by

T. S. TOWERS.

(Twenty-two pieces)

A
Chest of
Old Songs

Northwall, Sanday, Orkney.

1900.

A COLLECTION of OLD SONGS.

I. — Miss Watson.

Key D. Allegro

{ :m.f|s :s|f :m|d|r :r|d :d.d|r :r|r :f.s|l}
{ :s| s :m.s|l||W| :d',l|s :d'|m :r|d| :m.f|s}
{ :s|f :m.d|r :r|d}

Miss Betsy Watson is my name,
I have brought myself to disgrace & shame
By loving a young man that ne'er
lov'd me,
My folly now I plainly see.

II. — Poor Old Worn-out Sailor.

Key Eb. Scots ... Slow

{ :d|m :s||l :t|d' :s|m :d|m :s||l :t|d'|,l :t|d',t}
One summer eve all labour o'er & finds were sweetly singing,
I pitied his sad mournful tale for fully ám no sailor, When he —
When false reports came home I was dead my wife did ...

{ :l|l —s :m|d :r|m||t|d :r|r :m|r :d|d}
heard his far worn out village tho' our village came a begging
show your charity said he on a poor old worn out sailor /
daughter ran / I knew not where, forevermore to be parted.

PREFACE.

In preparing this small book, I have
strictly confined myself to the object
I had in view, namely to put into music
some old songs, which I had often
heard sung, but which I had never
seen on paper.

It is very probable that a
number of errors may have been
made; corrections of these will be
thankfully received. T.S.T.

Contents.

Figure 3   T.S. Towers's Manuscript showing the first three pages

A good many comic or satirical local verses, not necessarily intended to be sung, still circulate on manuscript sheets in Orkney and Shetland. The most remarkable case is 'Laxo's Lines', a satirical epic in twelve 'cantos' about an amorous Shetland laird in the early eighteenth century, attributed to a clerical student, which circulated covertly for two and a half centuries in this form. I borrowed a typescript copy in 1974, not long before it was published by Thuleprint under the title of *Shetland Scandals*.

Clearly manuscript sheets function in much the same way as broadsides used to. Broadsides were certainly sold in Orkney, not only on occasions like the Lammas Market in Kirkwall, but apparently by chapmen who went round all the islands with a variety of wares. William Thomson in North Ronaldsay told me of a farm worker in that remote island less than a century ago who bought a chapbook of John Burness' verse tale 'Thrummy Cap' from a packman and took a whole day off work to learn the words, so that he was known as 'Thrummy' ever after. That poem may not have been sung, but the 48-verse 'The Turkey Factor' was, and Mr Thomson gave me a copy he had written from his memory of his mother's singing (he does not sing himself). He had been going to send it to an Orkneyman who had left the islands— but he would write him another, he said: so a song which no doubt reached Orkney as a broadside left it in 1967 as a manuscript sheet. One of the songs which everyone in Orkney used to know was 'Andrew Ross', the story of the brutal murder at sea of a simple-minded Orcadian sailor by bullying shipmates under a Captain Rogers. Captain Rogers and his mates were convicted of the murder at Liverpool assizes in August 1857. Apparently 'the strength of feeling in the crowd was remarkable' and so naturally a ballad was written on the subject, no doubt by some ballad-printer's hack in the north of England, though I remember no imprint when the late Ernest Marwick showed me his copy of the broadside. The details of this case I owe to Mrs Elizabeth Blackman from East Sussex, a descendant of a Ross family from Orkney, who looked up the trial reports in *The Times*. There is some suggestion that the crew were antagonised by Ross's evangelistic religion, but the report merely says he was 'apparently half witted and dirty in his habits'. A related story Ethel Findlater had heard, melodramatic but quite plausible, was that Ross's sister knew nothing of his fate until she heard someone singing the ballad.

Broadsides continued to circulate in Orkney and Shetland until remarkably recently. Charles Sanderson of Montrose Terrace, Edinburgh, was still advertising them in *The Scotsman* until about 1946. He sent catalogues and ballads in the 1940s to two Orcadians, Miss Helen Tulloch and John George Halcro, who lent them to me to copy. Peter Cooke has met people in Whalsay who also sent to Sanderson for ballads. As the catalogue confirms, he still charged the traditional 1d. per sheet (plus postage, I think), and had a great range of titles from 'Chevy Chase' to Harry Lauder's songs, with a special list of 'the favourite songs in country districts'. Many of the sheets are narrow slips printed by Sanderson himself or his father (?) whose shop was in the Canongate. However, some are two-column broadsheets or garlands of several pages, and the type-styles suggest some may have been printed a century before. Most of these bear no imprint, but some are from Glasgow and the Dundee 'Poet's Box', whereas others were printed in London by Fortey, Such, and Catnach.

Songs which became popular in the Northern Isles came from very far afield in some cases. The ballad about the shipwreck of the Dunbar in Australia had an Orkney connection, I was told—the captain was a South Ronaldsay man—but any song about a shipwreck seems to have moved an Orkney audience: I know of no such connection in the case of the Cospatrick, an emigrant ship which caught fire on the way to New Zealand, the Northfleet, another emigrant ship run down in the Channel, the Middlesex Flora wrecked on the coast of County Down, or the Ramillies on the coast of Devon. The last two were old established songs, but the other two are late Victorian tragedies with a sensational element to sell them—the few survivors of the Cospatrick were driven to cannibalism in their lifeboat (Palmer 1973, 40), and there was great public indignation because the Northfleet was run down by a foreign steamer which did not stop: I have actually seen three different songs on this subject which reached Orkney, two in manuscripts and one on a broadside. For some reason one of the songs which was known everywhere in Orkney was a sentimental ballad always called 'The Two Soldiers', which came from the American Civil War (Laws A17, 'The Last Fierce Charge'). It may have come by way of Canada, where many Orcadians worked in 'the Nor'-Wast' for the Hudson's Bay Company. However, I am not sure if this explanation can account for the presence of the typical American country version of the 'Frog's Courtship', complete with the 'M-hm' refrain, a black snake in place of the drake, and 'I wouldn't marry the President', which Mrs J.J. Leith picked up in

Harray about 1913 from an aunt who had heard it from someone in the neighbouring parish of Birsay—she seemingly noticed nothing strange about it.

Equally strange things happened with those 'Orkney songs' which Orcadians were so proud of. The pride of Ethel Findlater's repertoire was a song set at the prehistoric site in Stenness, 'The Ballad of the Standing Stones' (see Figure 1), with all the ingredients of melodrama—rival lovers, a stabbing, the appearance of the ghost and the death of the girl from 'a distracted mind'. Mrs Leith identified this for me as a youthful work of the Orcadian antiquary John Mooney, from a book of poems locally printed which, she tells me, he later tried to buy back and suppress. Ethel apparently got a copy, not quite complete, in manuscript, with the information that it could be sung to 'The Ploughboy's Dream', a tune she knew. She put them together and sang them at concerts with her husband, and her daughter still sings the song to great local admiration. Ethel evidently did not like having words of a song without a tune. 'Barbara Allen' was one case, where she eventually set her Scottish set of words to the best-known English tune, learned from an English soldier stationed in Orkney during the last World War. She could not get a tune to 'The Farmer's Boy' and finally made up her own, which proved to be an unconscious adaptation of 'The Two Soldiers' from 6/8 to 4/4 time. In another case she had an old newspaper cutting from her mother of a ballad about another local tragedy, as lurid as Mooney's and no doubt likewise founded on an existing legend: 'The Hamars of Syradale', named from an inland cliff off which one of the characters jumped. Ethel gave this a rather fine pentatonic tune which as far as I know is entirely original. A third such ballad to which she never learned the tune, though she had it in sol-fa with the words in a cutting from *The Orcadian* many years before, was 'Hoy's Dark Lofty Isle'; a sailor on his way back from the Greenland whaling dies within sight of land and his beloved Mary's home. Local tradition in Hoy, according to Isaac Moar, the late postmaster, identified Mary as a local woman whose house was pointed out, though in fact the song does not say that she lived in Hoy, just that she was near when the island, the first part of Orkney to come in sight from the sea to westward, was sighted. At any rate the song was widely known throughout Orkney, usually to a rocking 6/8 tune with the last of the three couplets repeated; but a tune brought to North Ronaldsay, said to be learned from a Hoy man a hundred years ago, is quite different, a little like 'Linden Lea', and does not repeat the words.

The circulation of songs in writing can then be considered a stimulus to musical invention. But songbooks, though they might be borrowed by a friend, or left to a sister by her emigrating brother, were not primarily a means of spreading songs around like songsheets and broadsides. Why did people compile songbooks? The obvious answer seems to be to help them to remember songs, and this was certainly the case with singers like Anna Taylor. Others I have recorded who had not been used to singing, at least recently, and did not have notebooks to consult though they remembered songs, always had to have the words written out before they would sing a song for me: but of those who gave me most, David Work in Shapinsay was well over 80 and could be forgiven for doubting his memory, and Mrs Leith in Stenness preferred to read from a written text even when telling a story and took ten years to acquire total confidence in front of a microphone. Ethel Findlater had no such need of her notebook: when Hamish Henderson dropped in on us on the first evening of her only visit to Edinburgh it was still in her case, and though she would really rather have gone for it, with Hamish's encouragement she went on to sing the whole of 'Lord Lovel' and nearly all, if not all, the fifty-five verses of 'Andrew Lammie'. But not everyone had her memory or love of songs, as I found in 1971 when she took me and Violet Manson to Finstown to call on Joe Linklater. She had learned from him 'The Dowie Dens of Yarrow' (see Figure 1), when he was a young ploughman on the next farm about 1914, or a version of it, for in 1969 she had told me her source for the ballad was her cousin Bella. Not only had he totally forgotten the song, but his wife told us that she had never heard him sing in fifty years of marriage. How much this was due to a changed atmosphere in Orkney after 1918, and how much to a feeling that an interest in songs was something for young unmarried people is hard to tell, but there is no doubt that many others who had been singers ceased to be, and it seems reasonable to suggest that if Joe Linklater had compiled and kept a songbook he would have been able to recall the ballad with its help.

It may be that songs were written down to save the effort of memorising the words. One important example, though hard to interpret, is the case of Peter Pratt in the East Mainland of Orkney. I visited him in 1966 before I saw Ethel, without any expectation of recording songs; Peter, then approaching the age of 87, was well known in Orkney as a player of the penny whistle, but people who knew him quite well and had played with him have told me since that they never heard him sing. Elisabeth Nielsen, a Danish fieldworker who visited Orkney and Shetland in the late summer of 1961, visited him twice and the first time recorded only tunes on the whistle and information on children's games—the latter was her central interest. It seems to have been only some way through her second visit that he offered songs, starting with three, 'Greenland' (*Tocher* 22, p. 232), 'Hoy's Dark Lofty Isle' and 'The Two Soldiers' in full, and sixteen further songs represented on the tape usually by only one verse. Obviously he had provided the rest of the words in another form, and in 1971 he told me that, thinking he would not be needing it again, he had given Elisabeth Nielsen his manuscript songbook to take away. In 1966, when I knew nothing of this, he volunteered to sing after some whistle-playing and gave me three songs: his own favourite, 'The Painful Plough' and 'The American Stranger', which he had sung in 1961, and 'The Blacks on India's Shore', which he had not. This last, which Roy Palmer has identified as a song of the Sikh Wars which appeared on broadside (*Scottish Studies* 14, p. 85; Palmer 1977, 196), he seems to have remembered complete, in seven long stanzas, from hearing it sung once at a dance in the village of Holm (St Mary's) five miles from his home when he was in his teens, seventy years before. In 1971 I asked him about the songs he had given Ms Nielsen and played the verses he had recorded of 'The Sheffield Apprentice' and 'A Sailor and his True Love', but he said he had forgotten these. On a second visit he recorded 'Jamesie Brine' (nine verses, without the first—recorded in 1961—which was too like the beginning of 'The Blacks on India's Shore'), and he sang 'The Painful Plough' once more, but otherwise he sang me different songs that year. These seem to have been brought to his mind by other vaguely similar songs from a tape of Orcadian singers I played him. They included three complete songs, one of them 'The Old Ramillies' (*Tocher*, 3, p. 90; Palmer 1973, 38). He had some difficulty in recalling the beginning of verse two, but got it later. Two of the new items recorded in 1971 were a fragment of 'Bold Dighton' (Laws A21) and 'Pat McCarthy' (Laws K26), songs better known in North America which Peter might well have picked up when he spent some years in Canada in his thirties, probably after his manuscript was written. 'Pat McCarthy' is in the manuscript of his neighbour George Low, but George certainly learned some songs from Peter. Obviously his memory was good for a man of 92, but some of the songs he knew best seem not to have been in the manuscript (or did Ms Nielsen not have time to record them? She had room on the tape for more recordings made the same day), and he does not seem to have remembered many of those in the manuscript well. Some of them were popular rather than traditional songs, including 'The Rose of Tralee' and 'Mother Kissed Me in my Dream', but this did not necessarily influence his choice; though he knew in 1971 that I was looking for 'old' songs, one fragment he sang then was 'Break the News to Mother'.

The songs recorded in a notebook, it seems, need not be the same that were remembered and could be sung. It was not easy to question Peter Pratt on how he memorised texts, but it seems likely that he sang these songs to himself, at the plough, even if he seldom or never sang in company. The characteristic use of a notebook was perhaps to record any new song that had just been heard, whether or not it was intended to be memorised and sung. Few of the people I found with songbooks had ever sung in public, though before 1920, when it was normal practice, they might have ventured a song or two at New Year or some small gathering in a neighbour's house. Whereas it would not be surprising to find that, as on the manuscript songsheet or 'ballat' of an Irish rebel song reproduced by Henry Glassie (Glassie 1982, 58), 'Stanzas are not divided into lines, but break when the melody repeats', in fact nearly all Orcadian examples are divided into lines. On small sheets these may often overrun and would therefore prove awkward to sing from as certainly the Irish example would. Although 'spellings reveal that the text was written from memory or taken from dictation', as with our 'Ghostsport' instance, in Orkney at least dialect spellings are rare, because the writers were taught to write standard English at school and had the example of the broadsides to follow. As on song-slips Scots is confined to self-consciously 'Scotch' songs and a few words in older ballads, and is spelt more or less as the writer heard it apart from a few well-known conventions. Alternatively it may be Anglicised: George Low writes 'cow or ewe' for 'coo or yowe'. Ethel Findlater's more recent manuscript has more Scots forms than most, and nearly always points them out with inverted commas for the more unusual words and a personal code of an apostrophe following any dialect word—a generalisation from *wi'* and *comin'* to *tae'* and *ye'* also. *Oh'* likewise has an apostrophe, probably by confusion with *o'* for *of.* Sometimes she is phonetic (*our* for *ower*), and uses one or two forms which Orcadians regard as part of their own dialect (*me* for *my*, which several manuscripts have, and *wae* for *wi'*), but more often she will write a Scots form (*dae* for *do, guid* for *good*) although she usually sang the native Orkney form (*dö, göd*, spelt according to Orcadian convention *deu, geud*).

Song notebooks, then, are not primarily designed as aids to singing, though they could be useful for memorising songs, and their presence may have served sixty years ago as it certainly does for some now as a psychological prop—not much used to prompt the singer's memory, but like taking an umbrella to prevent it raining. Even in the much less literate Gaelic culture of the Highlands one hears of singers who will not perform without a printed book, but may hold it upside down; it adds authority. However, the notebooks seem to have been first and foremost collections—like a stamp collection or a scrapbook, a point endorsed by Jim Carroll and others at the conference. (I think it was Jim Carroll who mentioned seeing a song torn out of someone's book to give to a visitor who wanted it, like swopping stamps.) They also function like the collections of broadsides to which in a sense they are successors. You collected everything you could that came your way, for I have seen little evidence of specialised collection, apart from a tendency to stick to the older songs, a situation which may have been dictated mainly by the difficulty in getting recent London hits in Orkney before 1914. Once the collection was made, favourites could be selected and learnt if you were a singer, just as some records in a record collection may be played far more often than others. If you were not a regular singer in public, as probably the majority of collectors were not, you could still learn songs to sing to yourself and perhaps bring out occasionally at a party where everyone had to do something. Moreover, a collection of songs written in your own hand and learned mostly from friends and neighbours was a more personal thing than a collection of stamps or broadsides—rather like an autograph album, but more interesting. Notebooks, unlike broadsides or single songs in manuscript, were the static end product of song transmission and seldom played much part in further transmission, though for the student they are valuable evidence of the repertoire that was circulating where and when they were written.

References

Bruford, Alan,
   1974,   'The Grey Selkie', *Scottish Studies* 18, pp. 63-81.
Child, Francis James,
   1882-98   *The English and Scottish Popular Ballads*, Cambridge, Mass.:
             Houghton, Mifflin and Company, reptd edn 1965, New York:
             Dover.
Glassie, Henry,
   1982,   *Passing the Time in Ballymenone*, Dublin: O'Brien, and Philadelphia:
             University of Pennsylvania Press.
Henderson, Hamish,
   1983,   'At the foot o' yon excellin' brae: The Language of Scots Folksong',
             Scotland and the Lowland Tongue, ed. J.D. McClure, Aberdeen:
             Aberdeen University Press, pp. 100-28.
Laws, G. Malcolm,
   1964,   *Native American Balladry*, revd edn, Philadelphia: American
             Folklore Society.
Ord, John,
   1930,   *The Bothy Songs and Ballads*, Paisley: Alexander Gardner.
Palmer, Roy,
   1973,   *The Valiant Sailor*, Cambridge: Cambridge University Press.
   1977,   *The Rambling Soldier*, Harmondsworth: Penguin.
Shuldham-Shaw, Patrick,
   1976   'The Ballad "King Orfeo"', *Scottish Studies* 20, pp. 124-26.

SONG AND HISTORY*

Dave Harker

This paper will not be about particular songs or how they can be related to what happened in history, so much as about one method of developing the discussion of the relationship between songs and history in a learning situation. I have attempted to use and to develop the application of this method on three occasions, using a particular song-text, 'The Original Bob Cranky', and the results of these experiments and my own research have appeared in the 1985 *Folk Music Journal*, so I will not duplicate that work here. I will, however, try to spell out the problems I met and the solutions I attempted. The first occasion I tried to use a different approach was at the September 1982 weekend symposium organised at Exeter by the International Association for the Study of Popular Music (IASPM), entitled 'Popular Music Research in the U.K.: Concerns and Responsibilities'. The second experiment was carried out on unsuspecting people at the EFDSS/IDFLS conference at Leeds in November 1982; and the third was at the November 1983 History Workshop 17, 'Industrialisation—and After', held in Manchester. I would like to thank the people who invited me—namely, David Horn, Ian Russell, and Paul Salveson—and especially those dozens of people who thought they were going to be talked at when they came in, but who entered into the spirit of the experiment with comradeliness and no little erudition. It seems to me to be one of the chief merits of this method that it has proved suitable for groups of people of varying sizes—from a dozen or so to seventy—and of varying levels of knowledge—from professors to people with only a marginal interest in the subject. I also believe that the method is applicable to an almost

*This paper provides an overview to a series of three Workshops I organised, one of which was at the 'Traditional Song' conference at Leeds, 20 November 1982.

infinitely wide range of issues, given adequate preparation on the part of the tutor and a willingness to participate actively on the part of the workshop.

What I am about to describe are essentially problem-centred learning methods, using small groups and plenary sessions. I claim no originality for these methods, which have been in use for over sixty years in some educational institutions. In fact, I came to them rather late, as part of a change of line by the Trades Union Congress Education Department on how they wanted their sponsored shop stewards' courses run. However, at the time when I began using the problem-centred method in relation to the analysis of songs, I knew of no-one else who was doing so, and it felt to me to be an innovation, albeit a modest one. I wanted to use these methods for certain very clear reasons. Firstly, I hate conferences, and above all the competition and general point-scoring which seems to be built into them. Secondly, I occasionally get asked to conferences, so I have the option either of refusing the invitations (and offending people) or of making an effort to marginalise the effects of careerism, brow-beating and the 'expert' syndrome. Thirdly, from my own experience on the receiving-end of lectures, talks, and papers, I know just how boring, alienating, and non-productive (in an intellectual sense) such academic forms of cabaret are, and how patronising it is to feel you have a contribution to make, or a question you badly want to ask, when only a token five minutes are left for discussion at the end of an hour's jawing. It seems to me that the traditional academic format is designed to suppress discussion, and that even its nominally more liberal variant, the seminar, is so often a series of short and equally suppressive lectures. In academic jargon, the thing becomes tutor-centred rather than student-centred, and the client relationship which this involves links neatly to the power relationship which is built-in to academic institutions at all levels. Quite what this has to do with learning is problematical, to say the least, but of course this traditional method fits perfectly into the hierarchical, elitist, and generally unpleasant social relations characteristic of western 'democracies' and of eastern 'socialist countries'.

When I planned the Exeter session (which was to be an hour and a quarter with about forty people) I had no illusions about being able to transcend the real relations of educational production, but I hoped what I was trying to do would in some ways subvert or at least show up the strangeness of what normally happens. I overprepared, probably out of anxiety, so that each person present received not only a substantial two-part 'bibliography of folksong and related materials', entitled 'Song and History' (since published as an IASPM internal publication at Göteborg in 1983), but also a set of my own notes on what I termed the decoding of the particular song in question, another version of that text (with printed music), a chronology of the nineteenth century manuscript and printed variants, and a set of working propositions about the relationship between songs and history. All this was delivered at the end of the session, my aim being to show that scholars interested in song and those interested in workers' culture and history had to forge links and to develop methods collaboratively. (The politics of this, quite simply, were to stress the need for IASPM to recognise that popular music did not begin in 1956, but had a modest history of some centuries before that apocalyptic date.) What happened in the previous session was that everyone was given a song-text in its manuscript form and they were asked, verbally, to consider what information they would need to understand the text historically. Truthfully, the group size was too large. There were some problems with language, and not only those experienced by colleagues from overseas, given the 'Geordie' idiom of the song! And some people were unhappy about offering experience or posing questions on a subject which most of them found quite interesting but slightly peculiar. All in all, the Exeter pilot venture was a qualified disaster, in terms of learning about the song in question, but the kinds of questions which did come up, during and especially *after* the end of the session, indicated that there were possibilities for developing and structuring a session in a better way. People were able to get through the individualistic wall to some extent, and to raise questions about vocabulary, dialect, provenance, date, authorship, authenticity, stereotypes, structure, historical 'markers', function, form, and suchlike in what promised to be a co-operative and fruitful fashion. But then the time ran out!

Learning from this disorienting experience—I was never quite sure where the discussion was going—I prepared differently for Leeds. This time, the seventy people in the room had a very brief introduction, were asked to form into groups of four, and then to work on an activity—see Appendix 1—which sought to set out the aims of the exercise, to structure the group discussion by breaking the task into coherent sections, and to enforce some collective discipline by introducing a time (which, inevitably, was insufficient). Given the madness of attempting report-backs from around fourteen groups, it was still possible to accumulate on a blackboard some of the main questions that needed to be asked of the text, the appropriate sources and a few stabs at analysing the text as an historical document; but, once again, time ran out in between stage two and stage three of the process, and some of us felt that the whole thing remained firmly up in the air, even though many of my prepared documents were distributed at the close. The real challenge to the formal educational mode was recognised—A.E. Green later wrote to tell me that a comrade from the People's Republic of China had found the experience interesting—and feedback from later contributions and members of their audience suggested to me that the different approach brought out the problems inherent in talking and being talked at as a form of teaching/learning. Clearly, however, I'd still not got it right, and after a year's gestation I made a third attempt.

This time, I not only specified a maximum workshop of twenty people to the Workshop organisers, but I also asked for a room which would hold twelve to sixteen people comfortably, with four tables for the small group work. (I think about twelve to fourteen came.) I took five minutes to set out my approach, get people's consent, and organise the groups. Since I knew only a couple of people, I couldn't arrange for a mix of more and less experienced people to be in each group, as I would have wished; but other organisational details were better-prepared. People had flip-charts and pens, tables to write on, a shorter and clearer activity sheet (see Appendix 2), a little more time—though I stressed the need for rigid discipline—and more manageable groups of between three and five people (the large ones had absorbed late-comers). The whole thing worked much more smoothly, organisationally, and I felt that the report-backs from the groups, the attempts at analysis and then synthesis, and the summing-up by the tutor were quite productive, given that this was a one-off session involving people most of whom did not know each other when they came through the door.

Of course, there were problems. For example, groups tended to select the hoariest-headed or the most extrovert person to chair discussions, and this seemed to lead to an element of orthodox tutoring inside the groups. One group reporter cheerfully ignored the decisions taken by his colleagues, and gave us his version of what the song-text signified. At the end of the session, there was a determined move to get the tutor to offer his considered analysis, as if to check convergences and points of difference—'did we get it right?', 'you're supposed to be the expert', 'earn your money' (there wasn't any!) and suchlike unspoken sentiments lay behind this pressure. What was really going on, of course, was a re-emergence of deeply-held ideas about hierarchical educational procedures, for all the comradely policing of individualism that had gone on during most of the hour and a half. People—and even socialists—really do find it difficult to accept a tutor in a role different to that of 'floor manager' or 'conductor of the orchestra', equipped with a score or a script which they have carefully prepared, and on which they are meant to lean heavily. In truth, the feeling of insecurity engendered in a tutor who does not know what ideas might come out of group work seems to me to be one of the most stimulating things about the whole process. Why should one person know everything, or pretend to? Why should not someone in a workshop that is *really* a *work*shop know more than the nominal tutor? Why do we insist on a mode of educational production which is almost completely effective in stifling real discussion? How do people really learn? This last question—one of some importance in a rational world—seems to me to be the one issue which is systematically ignored in most teaching/learning situations. The question is sometimes reduced to a set of techniques, or to a strategy based on external constraints (such as a syllabus or an examination), but the underlying ideological assumptions are rarely teased out or examined. So let me be perfectly open about the ideas which seem to me to underpin the problem-centred small-group methods which I have briefly described.

First of all, these methods assume that people are not unintelligent, and that everyone has some experience or knowledge or skills to contribute. Secondly, they assume that people learn not by being told, talked at, or whatever by some 'expert'. (A shop steward once defined an 'expert' as follows: '"x" is an unknown quantity, and a "spurt" is a drip under pressure'.) People learn through experience, activity, and, in a general sense, struggle. Further than this, most people do not learn by somehow absorbing abstract ideas and then going away to apply those ideas. Instead, they proceed from their concrete knowledge and experience, through engagement in activity, towards an understanding of what they are studying in abstract terms, and *then* they test that understanding back onto whatever concrete reality is appropriate. For example, they might look at a song-text, discuss it collectively and reach certain tentative conclusions, and then go back to that text and others in order to test the validity of their abstract ideas. This process is not a fixed or final one, of course: usually, before general ideas can be developed, a lot of checking procedures come into play, as between (in this case) a particular song-text and such tentative ideas about it as have been reached in any given time. In the case of 'The Original Bob Cranky', for example, people wanted dialect dictionaries, parallel texts, variant texts, information about authors, places, pit-work, periods, and so on; and, in a more extended educational process, such documents would be sought, used and the results applied, as in the article which has now been produced. This leads to another important element in the application of these methods—one which has far-reaching consequences— that is, the attempt to analyse by the use of a thesis, its antithesis, and a period of struggle towards a synthesis. This is sometimes known as the dialectical method.

What the use of a problem-centred activity achieves—if it's properly thought out and related to the needs of the learners and the aims of the session or course—is to bring out thesis, antithesis, and some sort of provisional synthesis. For example, at the Leeds conference the blackboard became full of issues relating both to the content of the song- text, and to a very wide range of issues relating to the culture (and the economic system) in which that text was produced. People wanted to know not only about working methods in NE pits around 1800, but about how and why those techniques were changing. This, in turn, led on to the question of underlying economic factors, such as the market for coal, the development of coal-using technology, and the capitalisation of the coal industry. Other avenues for information-gathering were opened up, but in the confines of half an hour's report-back and discussion even this part of the task was not manageable, and there was absolutely no chance of following the questions through by going to other primary and secondary sources. To do that, in a less inflexible learning situation—as part of a course, for example—you would need some form of information bank of relevant materials, and a small library (or ready access to one), which would have to be built up by tutors in the first instance, but added to according to learners' needs and queries as the work developed. This, of course, is a counsel of perfection; but it can be done—I have helped build up such an Information Bank for the shop stewards' courses held in Manchester, and now the stewards help not only to maintain it, but also to keep it up to date.

In the end, the use of a method like the one described depends on whether or not it achieves its aims as set out in the activity sheet, and whether those aims are the ones the tutors want to achieve. If tutors want to involve people, draw on their experience, skills and knowledge, and make some effort towards collective learning (which includes the tutor), I can claim wholeheartedly that this method works. In fact, though I did a considerable amount of individual research work in order to write the *Folk Music Journal* article, it is perfectly true to say that I learned something new at each of the three workshops, and that the analysis was pushed further and the synthesis clarified. It is my belief that the second activity could be used not only with any song-text (music as well as words, for those with the technical competence which I lack), but with poetry, prose, and, indeed, almost any kind of artistic production. And it would work. The fundamental issue, then, is not whether problem-centred learning achieves its aims, but whether people really want those aims to be achieved.

APPENDIX 1

Decoding 'The Original Bob Cranky': An Activity

Aims: To help us understand the problems of using songs as historical evidence

To help us analyse the problems of writing history using only orthodox sources

To develop a method of interrogating song-texts in the absence of sound-recording and musical evidence

To help us understand the problems involved in the mediation of song-texts

To help us consider the importance (or otherwise) of a consistent theoretical approach

Task: In your groups, elect someone to chair the discussion, and another person to take notes and report-back to the meeting.

Examine the song-text you have been given and, very quickly, make a list of the questions you would need to be able to answer in order to feel you understood enough about the provenance of the text. Give one example of each kind of problem which prompts your questions.

Make a list of the kinds of historical sources which you might expect to be of use in understanding this text historically. Give any particular examples your group knows.

At first sight, what do you take to be the significance of this song-text in terms of the history and culture of labouring people?

Timing: 20 minutes.   (Please try to spend at least the same amount of time on each question.)

APPENDIX 2

Song and History: An Activity

Aims: To help us think about the problems involved in using song-texts as sources for writing history

To help us begin to develop a methodology for analysing song-texts

To help us practise working collectively

Task: In your small group, elect someone to chair your discussion, and another person to take notes and transfer your findings on to flip-charts.

Look at the song-text you have been given, and list all the questions you would want answered in order to be able to understand the text.

List the sources you would use in order to answer these questions (either specific sources, or some indication of the kind of source).

Using the information you can think of now, try to analyse the text.

Put your responses to all three sections on separate flip-charts.

Time: 25 minutes

Resources: 'The Original Bob Cranky' manuscript text, your own knowledge and experience

A.L. LLOYD—A PERSONAL VIEW*

Leslie Shepard

There must be many people who were closer to Bert Lloyd than I was, but I am happy to open this tribute because we were of roughly the same generation. I too had working-class roots and came from a poor family, with no special schooling. Bert Lloyd has always been one of my heroes, in company with such people as the Revd Sabine Baring-Gould, the Revd Joseph Ebsworth, and folksinger John Jacob Niles, also original and highly talented pioneer folklorists.

I first came across the name A.L. Lloyd in 1937, with the publication of his splendid translation of Federico García Lorca's *Lament for the Death of a Bullfighter* (London: Heinemann). About that time, I was reading James Joyce's *Ulysses* and was fascinated by the poetry of Dylan Thomas and T.S. Eliot.

Even allowing for the basic qualities of Lorca himself, there is no mistaking the passion and beauty of Lloyd's translation. Perhaps more than any other work, this translation demonstrated the extraordinary dichotomy of his character—the wild romantic feeling for folk poetry, and on the other hand the brilliant analytical scholarship with a left-wing interpretation. That political flavour has often worried those of his contemporaries who, like myself, did not share his position. It tended to be either something you ignored or tried to explain away. If we are to understand this extraordinarily talented man, we have to see this against the background of his time.

Those who grew up in the thirties and forties now find it difficult to convey the dead hand of mediocrity and authoritarianism of those days. Britain was a class-ridden society with rigid barriers and social problems that nobody seemed to care about. The mainstream of art,

*This tribute was made at the opening of the 'A.L. Lloyd Memorial Conference', London, 4 February 1984, and was accompanied by a film from *Mining Review*, 1951, and by tape recordings from 1950.

A.L. Lloyd and Alf Edwards at a Centre 42 concert in 1962

Photo by Brian Shuel

literature, and poetry was largely conformist and snobbish. Even folk music was mainly a middle-class study. It is not surprising that new directions in art, literature, and social change tended to have a left-wing flavour, intensified by the drama of the Spanish Civil War and the fight against totalitarian Fascism.

Many talented intellectuals of that period experienced a political conversion equivalent to an irreversible religious experience. Only one or two intellectuals like Arthur Koestler and George Orwell saw the futility of swapping old dogmas for new ones. Few people could have foreseen a post-war affluence in which rigid class barriers melted away into a uniformly bourgeois society with upper and lower levels, in which a working-class bricklayer might be transformed into a property millionaire almost overnight, with a House of Lords stuffed with Labour Party peers.

During the 1930s, I had a dead-end job in an asbestos factory which ruined my lungs and in my spare time was a member of an amateur film society. Through the initiative of my professional film director friend Jack Chambers, I joined Paul Rotha Productions in 1942, working on documentary films. We were all a bit left-wing in those days. Documentary films were to deal with the creative interpretation of reality, and for most of us that meant the idealisation of factory workers for the war effort and a constant theme of 'the people' co-operating to solve social problems and make Britain a better place to live in after the war.

Some of us seceded from Paul Rotha and formed Data Film Productions, a co-operative unit pledged to make films of social significance. From 1948 onwards, I managed a monthly news-film called *Mining Review*, sponsored by the National Coal Board, shown in cinemas throughout industrial areas. I directed items, scripted, assisted editing, wrote commentaries, and later became Associate Producer. This series became phenomenally successful, and long after I had left the film industry, it continued for an astonishing total of thirty-five years before being recently axed by the Coal Board.

During this period, I had met Bert at the house of Jack Chambers, together with Chalotte Ohly, who became Mrs Lloyd. I had already been tremendously impressed by Bert's first essay *The Singing Englishman*, issued as a 70 page pamphlet by the Workers' Music Association in 1944 at one shilling and sixpence old money (see Figure 1). It was, and I believe still is, the best introduction to the subject,

Some records of Folk Music

The Keys of Heaven (*arr. Broadwood*) – – – ANNE ZIEGLER and WEBSTER BOOTH	B9226
Haul Away, Joe ; What Shall We Do with the Drunken Sailor ? – – – – – – **Fire Down Below ; Hullabaloo Balay** – – –	B2420
Shenandoah ; Rio Grande and **Billy Boy** – – – JOHN GOSS and Male Voice Quartet	B2646
Handkerchief Dance (Country Gardens) (*Grainger*) – MARK HAMBOURG	B4437
Brigg Fair (*Delius*) – – – – – – **Fantasia on Sea Shanties** – – – – LONDON SYMPHONY ORCHESTRA	D1442–3 C2452
Road to the Isles ; Skye Boat Song – – – STUART ROBERTSON	B8260
Herding Song ; Eriskay Love Lilt – – – – JOSEPH HISLOP	DA789
Next Market Day ; I Have a Bonnet Trimmed with Blue – – – – – – – – – **I will Walk with my Love ; I Know where I'm Going** BARBARA MULLEN	B9132
Danny Boy (Londonderry Air) – – – – – WEBSTER BOOTH	B9022
Londonderry Air (*arr. Grainger*) – – – – NEW SYMPHONY ORCHESTRA	B2915

★ For Folk Dance Records see " *His Master's Voice* "
complete catalogue.

"HIS MASTER'S VOICE"
GREATEST ARTISTS - FINEST RECORDING

The Gramophone Company Ltd., Hayes, Middx.

Figure 1: An advertisement from *The Singing Englishman*, 1944, which lists gramophone recordings of concert style performances of arranged folk songs, demonstrates the backcloth against which the book was written.

notwithstanding Bert's expansion and development of *The Singing Englishman* into the 433 page *Folk Song in England* (London: Lawrence and Wishart) twenty-three years later.

The Singing Englishman was rapidly followed in 1945 by a 66 page booklet titled *Corn on the Cob: Popular and Traditional Poetry of the USA* at three shillings and sixpence. It was a fine selection with a perceptive introduction, lacking only the music for the songs.

You can imagine how honoured I was to meet Bert in person at the home of Jack and Gerda Chambers, and listen to his brilliant folklore anecdotes interspersed with unselfconscious folk singing. Even now I am still amazed by the vast erudition of that man and the range of his researches. I had come to English folk music via jazz, negro blues, hobo songs, Jimmie Rodgers the yodelling brakeman, broadside ballads, and the discovery that the English Folk Dance and Song Society had a genuine folk music recording of Harry Cox. Bert had been through the whole territory! He had even discovered folk singer Phil Tanner on the Gower peninsula.

At that time, the *Mining Review* film was fortunate in having as its Coal Board films officer Kurt Lewenhak, who was also interested in experimental theatre and knew Ewan MacColl and other folk singers. During the filming of *Mining Review* stories in the coalfields, I had come across evidence of industrial folklore, and I had the idea of doing a story in which Bert Lloyd would talk about the subject and ask miners to contribute folk songs. Jack Chambers and Kurt Lewenhak agreed, but first we thought it a good idea to do a sound test. So I borrowed the film unit's portable tape recorder and Jack arranged for Bert to give us another evening and record his singing.

In those days, tape recorders were something of a novelty, and this one was called portable simply because it had a handle. In fact, it weighed over fifty pounds. Moreover the tape of that period was a fragile *paper* tape coated with iron oxide. It is astonishing that those early tapes are still playable after more than thirty years.

I directed Bert's *Mining Review* appearance in 1951 in a tiny set at Carlton Hill Studios, Maida Vale ('The Miner Sings', *Mining Review*, no. 9, Fourth Year, May 1951). It was my first sound dialogue item. We linked the item to a competition in the Coal Board's magazine *Coal*. It was on the basis of response to this short film item that Bert later developed his book *Come All Ye Bold Miners: Ballads and Songs of the Coalfields* published in 1952 (London: Lawrence and Wishart).

I can't claim that I became a close associate of Bert. There was a certain enigmatic reserve about him and I suspected a secret sorrow. Maybe it was just the strain of making ends meet. We kept in touch. We exchanged letters and information. I approached him when I planned a recording trip to Harry Cox. I read practically everything Bert wrote and went to his first appearance at a skiffle concert, a kind of halfway house between folk music and jazz which eased us into the Folk Song Revival.

I think we are inclined to forget just how much the folk song revival of the fifties and sixties owed to the left-wing movement, although they sometimes bent tradition to breaking point and introduced a false note into folk song. I for one, could not stomach eulogistic ballads of Stalin, and I think that those who did have regretted it. But Bert Lloyd was never a doctrinaire propagandist. His political interpretations of history were his own, and arose from identification with the under-privileged of the world and a deep appreciation of their folklore an music. He did not allow his views to affect the precision of his scholarship, and anyone can read his books and form their own views. Remember, too, that at the other extreme, this was the era of McCarthyism and vicious political witch hunts, which all honest libertarians despised. It is easier today to see that political insight needs to be divorced from worn-out dogmas of right and left.

In 1959, there was something of a slump in documentary films and I left the industry. I went to India and spent a year living in an old temple on the banks of the River Ganges, in the foothills of the Himalayas, studying religious philosophy and Indian music. I hasten to add that this was years before the Beatles heard the sitar or the advent of mass media pop gurus.

Some time after I got back to England, I wrote my first book *The Broadside Ballad* (London: Herbert Jenkins, 1962). Bert was kind enough to read the typescript and make some useful suggestions. I particularly remember how tactful and generous he was to my inexperience and naiveté. He agreed to write a Foreword, which is a valuable little essay in itself. He obviously differed radically on the issue of my metaphysical approach to ballads, his own being that of social criticism, but his dissent was courteous and carefully worded, with a touch of good humour.

His own books are characterised by a clarity of expression and a forceful style, in which one can feel the scholar struggling with the romantic in his nature. For those who are interested in the bibliographical side of his work, let me give a few notes. With Igor Vinogradoff, he published *Shadow of the Swastika; A Radio-Drama in Six Parts of the Story of the German National Socialist Party* (London: John Lane, 1940). Together with his wife Charlotte, he translated *Answer in the Sky* by Dieter Meichsner (Funk and Wagnall, 1953, also issued by Putnam under the title *Vain Glory*). Some of you may remember the twelve issues of that splendid magazine *Recorded Folk Music* which Bert edited for Collet's from January 1958 to December 1959. In 1960, there was a slim volume of *Dances of Argentina* (published by Parrish). I have always regretted that I never bought a copy of his book *The Golden City* (London: Methuen, 1960) with illustrations by Pearl Binder. At the time it came out, I was a little disappointed to find that it was a children's book. In 1965, there was *Folk Songs of the Americas*, with I.A. de Rivera (London: Novello), and in 1967, of course, *Folk Song in England* (London: Lawrence and Wishart), followed by *The Penguin Book of English Folk Songs*, with Ralph Vaughan Williams (Penguin: Harmondsworth) in 1968. There were also many articles and erudite record sleeve notes.

His literary output may not be extensive, but it is rich in original thought and research. Much of the unique quality of Bert's insight lay in his personal contacts with the folk clubs, and those marvellous collecting trips in Eastern Europe, mainly issued by Topic Records. With Ewan MacColl, he also sang many of the items and contributed data to that remarkable series of nine L.P. records of the Child Ballads (*The English and Scottish Popular Ballads*) edited by my old friend Dr Kenneth S. Goldstein for Riverside Records. Bert clearly has a permanent memorial in his many records both as singer and collector, and I hope that some time somebody will prepare a complete discography of his recorded work.

I am very happy to say that through the courtesy of Francis Gysin, Films Officer of the National Coal Board, the copy of the *Mining Review* film of 1951, which contains that interview with Bert asking for coal-mining folk songs, has been presented to the archives of the English Folk Dance and Song Society. [The film was shown here.]

The thirty-three year old recordings of Bert at the house of my friend Jack Chambers in 1950 were made before Bert was performing widely in folk clubs. I think these songs somehow symbolise Bert's dual attitude of left-wing sympathy and love of traditional folklore. [Tape recordings of 'Nine Hundred Miles from my Home' and 'Which Side Are You On?' were played.]

I have always felt that it was precisely that left-wing label that prevented Bert from being honoured by any major academy for his unique contributions to folklore scholarship, although he did receive an honorary M.A. from the Open University in 1978. If anyone deserved the recognition of an honorary doctorate it was surely Bert Lloyd, although it might have embarrassed or even amused him.

I think he remains something of an enigma, expressing in himself the problem of folk music in a modern world geared to the lowest common denominator of pop culture. There was that light high speaking voice which changed magically to a strong baritone in singing, the desire for social change and the conservatism of tradition, a romantic at odds with a scholar.

Perhaps I could add, as epitaph, a few lines from Bert's wonderful translation of the Lorca's *Lament for the Death of a Bullfighter*, which was my first introduction to his work:

> But now he sleeps endlessly.
> Now mosses and grass
> are opening with sure fingers
> the flowers of his skull.
> And his blood goes singing now,
> singing by marshes and meadows,
> sliding on frozen horns,
> wavering soulless through the mist
> stumbling on its thousand hoofs
> like a long dark sad tongue. . .

A.L. LLOYD AND INDUSTRIAL SONG*

Roy Palmer

Bert Lloyd's interest in industrial songs dated back to some fifty years before his death. His experiences in the 1930s on Australian sheep farms and Antarctic whaling ships bore fruit much later in his Topic records, *Great Australian Legend* (12TS203, 1971) and *Leviathan* (12T174, 1967), and rather earlier in *The Singing Englishmen* (London: Workers' Music Association, 1944). This short book includes nine songs or parts of songs dealing with work at sea, of which three are directly concerned with whaling ('The Spermwhale Fisher', 'Greenland' and 'Blow Ye Winds'). Eleven songs are connected with agricultural life and work, covering such subjects as sheepshearing, poaching, ploughing, and protest. While traditional texts, sometimes with tunes, are normally given, on three occasions ('There's some that sing of the hiring fair', 'Come all you jolly ploughing boys that whistle through the fair', and 'What do you think of the ploughman now?'), Lloyd silently provides his own adaptations of items printed by John Ord in his *Bothy Songs and Ballads* (Paisley: Alexander Gardner, 1930) respectively 'The Weary Farmers' (p. 211), 'Swaggers', (p. 219), and 'The Braes o' Broo', (p. 254).

However, what we normally think of as industrial songs—those of extractive and manufacturing workers—are poorly represented in *The Singing Englishman*. Textiles provide only one song, the Luddite 'Foster's Mill' (p. 47). Lloyd must later have regretted, as many other things in a book affectionately remembered, but flawed, his comment that the songs of the Luddites were 'as wild, defiant, and unreasoning (in) character as the men themselves'. There is nothing on strikes or trade unionism, nothing on working conditions in mill and mine, nothing on working class life. Lloyd quotes a verse-appeal for funds for

*This paper was given at the 'A.L. Lloyd Memorial Conference', London, 4 February 1984.

A.L. Lloyd at the recording of 'The Iron Music' in 1962

the unemployed and comments: 'There is no point in quoting more than one of this kind of thing because they are so poor and so lacking in pride or passion or technique or beauty or even surprise that they do not qualify as folksong at all but as something else, though I am not sure what'. Clearly, in 1944 Lloyd's acquaintance with and admiration for industrial song remained in the future.

Only half a dozen years later he conceived the brilliant idea of making a collection of mining songs. He appealed to people in the mining communities through the journal, *Coal*, and film in *Mining Review*, for material to be sent to him. He later visited some of the correspondents. His collection appeared in 1952 as *Come All Ye Bold Miners* (London: Lawrence and Wishart). There were 66 items, of which 16 had tunes. I do not know whether the materials have been preserved among Lloyd's papers, but the information provided in the book on sources is often tantalisingly brief. To take just one example, the note on 'The Miner's Life' reads: 'Text from E.D. Williams, Brymbo, North Wales' (p. 132). Is this a printed text? If so, is it a broadside or from some other source? Is it a manuscript? If so, is it copied from elsewhere or taken down from oral tradition? If the latter, from whom did the informant obtain it? Such questions arise again and again, and they must remain unanswered. It is therefore fairly speculative to judge that 40 of the 66 items in the book come from printed song collections, eighteen from oral sources and only eight from broadsides.

Such categories are by no means watertight. For example, 'The Trimdon Grange Explosion' (p. 78) is 'As sung (one verse only) by R. Sewell, of Newcastle (1951). Remainder of text from J. Jefferson, Trimdon Grange, Co. Durham. From a ballad by Thomas Armstrong' (p. 136). Armstrong intended the song, which was published in his *Song Book* (1930), to be sung to the tune of 'Go and leave me if you wish it'. There were five verses which Lloyd silently reduced to four by dropping half of each of the original third and fourth verses and combining the residue as his third verse.

It is clear that Lloyd's editorial approach was not merely to reproduce the material sent to him. Sometimes the changes made were small, as with 'Trimdon Grange', but others were far-reaching. On 'Jimmy's Enlisted (or the Recruited Collier)' Lloyd laconically notes: 'Text from J.H. Huxtable, of Workington. A version of this ballad appears in R. Anderson's *Ballads in the Cumberland Dialect* (1808)'. In fact, the original is entitled simply 'Jenny's Complaint', and features not a miner

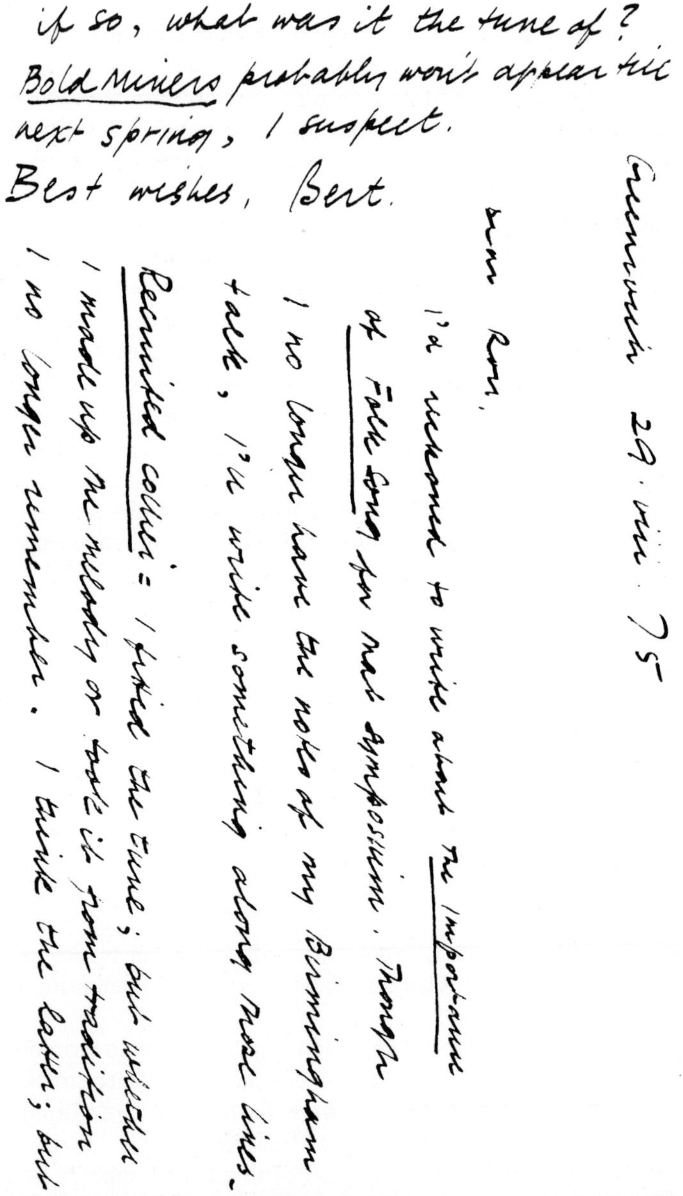

if so, what was it the tune of?
Bold Miners probably won't appear till
next spring, I suspect.
. Best wishes, Bert.

Greenwich 29. viii. 75

dear Roy,

I'd welcomed to write about the _importance_
of Folk Song for much symposium. Though
I no longer have the notes of my Birmingham
talk, I'll write something along those lines.

Recruited collier: I forget the tune; but whether
I made up the melody or took it from tradition
I no longer remember. I think the latter; but

Figure 1.   A.L. Lloyd to Roy Palmer 29 August 1975. The first paragraph refers
to Lloyd's essay, 'The Meaning of Folk Music' in _Folk Music in School_, edited by
Robert Leach and Roy Palmer (Cambridge, London, New York, Melbourne:
Cambridge University Press, 1978), pp. 5–28.

who enlists but a ploughman. A third party, Nicol, talks to Jenny about the wars, and Jemmy (as he is called) merely 'led' (carted) the coals which remind Jenny of him. Lloyd silently (and brilliantly) remade the song. Although one phrase, 'I'se leetin', sits uncomfortably in the new text the adaptation has enjoyed considerable success, to a tune also supplied by Lloyd to replace 'Nancy to the Greenwood Gane', which Anderson prescribed (see Figure 1).

'The Best-dressed Man of Seghill' (p. 91) was 'edited from a text communicated by J.S. Bell, of Whiston, Lancs.' (p. 137). Lloyd adds the information that 'the ballad was published as a broadside in April, 1831, with an engraving of a man tossed in a blanket'. A facsimile of this sheet, which was issued by J. Marshall of Newcastle, appears in Martha Vicinus, *Broadsides of the Industrial North* (Newcastle: Frank Graham, 1975, p. 46), as 'First Drest Man of Seghill, Or the Pitman's Reward for Betraying his Brethren—A New Song'. It bears these manuscript annotations, indicating the print run and the date of publication: '10 Quires March 31st 1831 Crown—3 on a sheet'. There are 15 verses of eight lines each, with a chorus indicated as 'With my fal la la, & c.' Lloyd prints only 12 verses, but in the second edition of *Come All Ye Bold Miners* (London: Lawrence and Wishart, 1978) he includes all 15, under the original title.

'The Coal-owner and the Pitman's Wife' (p. 93) was also from 'a text communicated by J.S. Bell', though a 'tune and fragment of the text' were separately supplied by J. Denison, of Walker (p. 137). The printed text was presumably the broadside without imprint in 12 verses with the title of 'The Old Woman and the Coal Owner'. It is interesting to compare this with the text given by Lloyd.

Broadside (1844)			Lloyd (1952)	
Verse 1	5 lines	=	Verse 1	4 lines
			Verse 2	? invented
Verse 2		=	Verse 3	
Verse 3		=	Verse 4	
Verse 4			Verse 5	

And the number is not known Sir, that is in that place	And the coal owners is the next on command
And they chiefly consist of the rich, wicked race;	To arrive in hell, as I understand,
And the Coal Owners are the next in command,	For I heard the old devil day as I cam out,
To arrive in h—l as I understand.	The coal-owners all had received their rout.

Verse 5
How know you the owners is next in command?
How div ah naw ye shall understand!
Aw hard the awd devil say when aw cam out
The Coal Owners all had received their rout.

Verse 6	=	Verse 6
Verse 7	=	Verse 9
Verse 8	=	Verse 7
Verse 9	=	Verse 8
Verses 10, 11, 12	=	Verses 10, 11, 12

So the changes made are in providing a new verse, in telescoping two old verses into one new, in altering the order of verses and in changing phraseology. The new second verse is a masterly invention, not only in keeping with but enhancing the spirit of the original. The other changes, particularly those in the order of verses, improve not only the flow of the piece, but its fervour. Lloyd's touch was sure, and his adaptations were invariably successful in performance. It is a pity that his lively singing of 'The Coal Owner' was not issued on a record.

As an editor he was keen to reconcile the page with the performance, and documentation with communication. It seems reasonable to suggest that he should have been more forthcoming with details of his editorial interventions.

Come All Ye Bold Miners created a stir of excitement when it appeared, and it quickly became a bedside book, not only for singers, but for miners. It was a pioneering book, the first collection of British mining songs, the first of British industrial songs. Twenty-six years later, in 1978, Lloyd published a second and enlarged edition, with 166 songs, of which 78 had tunes. This time, only six items came from printed song books. Broadsides (54), oral tradition (55) and composed songs (51) each provided roughly a third of the book. Of the last category thirty-one were of recent date, and many had been inspired by the book's first edition—something which was a source of considerable and justifiable pride in Lloyd. This was the folklorist intervening in folklore with a vengeance, but Lloyd's answer, had the suggestion been made to him, would surely have been that he considered himself part of the social and political scene, and not merely an observer of it.

A number of mining songs, including 'The Recruited Collier', sung by Anne Briggs, were included on *The Iron Muse: A Panorama of Industrial Folk Song arranged by A.L. Lloyd*, a record issued by Topic

(12T86) in 1963. In addition there were songs from other industries, such as textiles. One of these which later became widely known was 'The Weaver and the Factory Maid'. In response to an enquiry some years later Lloyd wrote: 'It is a composite piece made up of scraps from a version recorded by me from Mr William Oliver of Widnes, from Kidson's ms., and from a version copied by Mr Gale Huntington from the back of a ship's log-book' (personal communication, 16 March, 1967). Lloyd later communicated the Oliver text and Huntington the version from the Nellie (dating from 1769) (see Figure 2) and I printed them with others in my article, 'The Weaver in Love' (*Folk Music Journal*, 3 (1977), 261-74). Oliver's version had seven four-line verses, of which one lacked one line and two, two each. Lloyd dropped the original verse six and added two verses and two lines from the Nellie's log. There were also some changes of phraseology. For example, the more felicitous 'Her two Breasts standing so/Like two white hills . . . ' was substituted for 'her two breasts hanging so low/Like two white hills. . .'.

The *Iron Muse* was another pioneering venture with a widespread and lasting influence. In the accompanying leaflet Lloyd wrote that 'the folk songs of industrial workers have not been much noticed'. The record helped to change that. What were these songs? They were 'created by industrial workers out of their own daily experience and were circulated, mainly by word of mouth, to be used by the songmakers' workmates in mines, mills and factories'. 'That other branch of workers' song, made by learned writers and musicians on behalf of the proletariat and passed on chiefly through print is not represented on this record', Lloyd added.

The emphasis on distinguishing between print and orality, which Lloyd shared with Cecil Sharp and others, is repeated in *Folk Song in England* (London: Lawrence and Wishart, 1967). Industrial folk songs, he wrote, were 'the kind of vernacular songs made by the workers themselves directly out of their own experience, expressing their own interests and aspirations, and incidentally passed on among themselves mainly by oral means, though this is no *sine qua non*' (p. 317). Even in the same book Lloyd is moving away from the undue emphasis on orality. In the substantial chapter, about a quarter of the whole, devoted to industrial song he includes 41 items, of which 30 are not primarily from oral sources:

16 Crooms Hill   SE 10   7. vii. 71

Dear Roy,

I'm sorry not to have sent
this earlier. It was misplaced
in my file. I take the song
to be a re-make of at least
two earlier ones — one concerning
a humble servant girl (as in
the _Nellie_ version), the other
concerning a girl too stuck-up to
consort with weavers.

I'm not at all sure to what extent
I was justified in reconstituting
'my' version from the _Nellie_ one.
I wonder what 'Oldham' broadside
Mr Oliver had in mind. If a Bebbington one,
that's a bit late in the day. Was
Swindells' print shop in the Oldham
Road (they'd be about right for time)?

Best wishes
Bert.

Figure 2.   A.L. Lloyd to Roy Palmer, 7 July 1971

	broadside	composed	oral
textile	5	3	
mining	33	11	11	11
other	3	1	2	
	41	15	15	11

As we have seen, two thirds of the material in the second edition of *Come All Ye Bold Miners* also came from sources other than the oral tradition.

In a revised version of the *Iron Muse* leaflet Lloyd wrote: ' "Classical" folk song, music hall song, pop song, art song have all contributed to the home-made lyrical creations of industrial workers, but at heart the matter has remained astonishingly true to the tradition that, for want of a better name, we call "folk song" '. A further evolution in Lloyd's view was expressed in a lecture he gave in Birmingham on 13 September 1970. (I quote from my notes. A recording on the lecture is part of twelve hours of Lloyd preserved on tape in the Charles Parker Archive held at Birmingham Reference Library. Lloyd covered some of the same ground in his chapter, 'The Meaning of Folk Music', in the symposium, *Folk Music in School*, edited by Robert Leach and Roy Palmer (Cambridge: Cambridge University Press, 1978), pp. 5-28.) A differentiation was made between lyrical and more factual songs. The former, even when dealing with tragedy, like 'Johnny Seddon' or 'High Blantyre', Lloyd argued, provided little information. They were handsome in presentation but tended to be vague in detail and passive in mood. He related this to the rural tradition. On the other hand, the normal industrial approach was to provide an exposition of facts, to offer criticism and to express collective rather than individual truth. Such songs had to overcome the difficulty of stylising apparently non-poetical facts, but were frequently lively and humorous. The distinction again appears unduly sharp. A single event could inspire songs in both modes; a song in the second mode could evolve into the first; and a song might well contain passages in both modes.

Later in 1970 (letter dated 9 November) Lloyd sent me his proposed classification system for ballads of social event, which has remained unpublished and is given here as an appendix. He commented:

I've found it useful in ordering songs whose emphasis is rather what Americans call 'societal', as opposed to 'inter-personal'. Most of the English repertory *is* inter-personal—concerning love and loyalty, hostility and cruelty, trickery, flight and reunion between private individuals. But where this conflict is between person and social institution I feel a separate classification is called for and, as I say, I've found this one handy. Among other things, it helps us to winnow out Irish and Scottish themes and preoccupations. Of course, hardly any of our songs belong to a single thematic type; they mostly embody several narrative units, but still—even if only for cross-indexing—I find a 'social institutional' classification gets me out of some mazes.

Clearly, Lloyd's work in the field of industrial song is of major importance. He was prodigiously gifted both as a scholar and as a performer, and was a passionate communicator. There were influential innovations and insights in *The Singing Englishman*, *Come All Ye Bold Miners*, and *The Iron Muse*, not to speak of the many lectures, radio programmes, and other activities in which Lloyd was involved. *Folk Song in England* was another landmark.

Inevitably, there were shortcomings. Lloyd seems to have been slow to realise the immense importance of broadsides, and perhaps reluctant to move away from the classic view of the dominance of orality. The North-East occupied an unduly dominant place in his material, which perhaps accounts for the preponderance of mining songs in his books. Textiles were fairly well represented, but there was little from the metal trades, the potters, transport workers. A number of singer-writers, such as Joseph Mather of Sheffield, were neglected, and Lloyd seems to have recognised very late that certain aspects of music hall song were worthy of study.

Yet the balance sheet must be overwhelmingly on the credit side. The debts to Lloyd of almost anyone working in this field are enormous. What he said about the first edition of *Come All Ye Bold Miners* could be extended to the whole of his work on industrial song. The book, he wrote, 'had the effect of restoring to vigorous life many past songs, stimulating investigators to seek out lyrics dormant in cold corners of the memory of old miners and gathering dust in library cupboards, and best of all, encouraging members of miners' families to chance their arm at making songs for themselves about their own lives' (preface to second edition, p. 11). Bert Lloyd must take a fair measure of credit for the development that 'industrial folklore, thought to be a will o' the wisp, is taking on the proportions of an academic discipline as well as a cultural force' (p. 12).

Appendix

A Classification System for Ballads of Social Event (1970), by A.L. Lloyd (Primarily conflict-situations between persons and social institutions: armies, economic formations, political formations, the law. This system is not concerned with INTER-PERSONAL EVENTS—events in which the dramatic emphasis is upon essentially private encounters: family, lovers, friends, enemies).

1. ARMED CONFLICT ON SOCIAL-INSTITUTIONAL SCALE
    a. *Armed conflict: inter-group*
        Armed encounters between groups of persons which are neither individual nor national in scope.
    b. *Armed conflict: inter-nation*
        Armed encounters between self-defined 'nations' (including Scottish and Irish rebellions against England).
    c. *Armed conflict: separation*
        A person must depart from loved ones in order to serve in the armed forces of his country.
    d. *Armed conflict: injury*
        A person is injured while serving in his country's armed forces.
    e. *Armed conflict: death*
        A person is killed while serving in his country's armed forces.
    f. *Armed conflict: desertion*
        A person deserts from the armed forces of his country.
    g. *Armed conflict: flight*
        A person flees or departs in order to avoid armed conflict.
    h. *Armed conflict: arson*
        Combat takes the form of arson (setting fire to buildings occupied by the enemy) rather than with weapons.

2. ECONOMIC CONFLICT
    a. *Economic conflict: separation*
        A person must depart from loved ones in order to seek employment.
    b. *Economic conflict: hardship*
        Hardships are endured in the course of employment.
    c. *Economic conflict: injury*
        A person is injured in the course of his employment.
    d. *Economic conflict: strike or lock-out*
        A person withholds his labour, alone or in a group; or a person is locked out by his employer as a result of dispute.
    e. *Economic conflict: robbery*
        A person robs or steals from another person or from a social institution, *there being no personal relationship involving the robbery of the one by the other.**

f.   *Economic conflict: celebration*
A particular kind of employment is celebrated in narrative. (Generally, this does not involve a *conflict*, strictly speaking; though such ballads are not infrequently double-edged).

3.   POLITICAL CONFLICT
(POLITICAL CONFLICT and CIVIL CONFLICT are subdivided according to the punishment inflicted rather than the nature of the offence against society. In POLITICAL CONFLICT the offence is usually treason; in CIVIL CONFLICT it may be assassination, riot, assault, etc.)

a.   *Political conflict: exile*
A person accused of treason or other act against the state goes into exile.

b.   *Political conflict: imprisonment*
A person accused of treason or other act against the state is sent to prison.*

c.   *Political conflict: execution*
A person accused of treason or other act against the state is executed.*

d.   *Political conflict: reconciliation*
A person accused of treason or other act against the state effects a reconciliation with the authority concerned.

e.   *Political conflict: false accusation*
A person is falsely accused of treason or other act against the state.

*Ballads of the rescue of political prisoners may be worth considering as a subdivision, but these are more often in the form of INTER-PERSONAL EVENTS (Loyalty).

4.   CIVIL CONFLICT

a.   *Civil conflict: transportation*
A person is legally transported in punishment for an offence against civil authority.

b.   *Civil conflict: imprisonment*
A person is legally sentenced to imprisonment in punishment for an offence against civil authority.

c.   *Civil conflict: execution*
A person is legally executed in punishment for an offence against civil authority.

d.   *Civil conflict: armed conflict*
A person is killed, injured or dramatically involved in the course of an armed encounter with representatives of civil authority.

A.L. Lloyd and Ewan MacColl recording Radio Ballads

Photo by Brian Shuel

A.L. Lloyd the scholar—at his home in Greenwich, 1966

A.L. LLOYD AND HISTORY: A RECONSIDERATION OF ASPECTS OF '*FOLK SONG IN ENGLAND*' AND SOME OF HIS OTHER WRITINGS*

Vic Gammon

This conference is a testimony to the importance of A.L. Lloyd to folk song and related studies in this country. In this limited field Lloyd holds a position similar to that held by Raymond Williams in literary studies and E.P. Thompson or Christopher Hill in historical studies. The position is one of a major socialist intellectual who for a great number of people set the terms in which debates in these areas are conducted. Whether you agree with Lloyd's approach or not—and increasingly many of his assumptions and conclusions are being questioned—one cannot ignore it. Partly this is due to the paucity of his potential rivals. Who can read Karpeles or Howes trot out the tired clichés of the Sharp school with the pleasure that one can read A.L. Lloyd?[1] It is reputed that Mervyn Plunkett, one of the editors of *Ethnic* in the 1950s, wrote a large work on traditional music expressly criticising Lloyd's approach, but this was only read by a few and never saw the light of publication.[2] Younger writers, generally a product of the folk revival and a university education, have been slow to produce a sustained critique of Lloyd.[3] Even Dave Harker, trenchant critic of the ideologies of the folk song movement, began his paper on Lloyd in an uncharacteristically apologetic way when he delivered it here a year ago.[4] I must admit to some feelings of diffidence when I published my 'Song, Sex and Society' article in *Folk Music Journal* a couple of years ago. I found it hard to criticise a man who I felt had given me so much.[5]

We have to overcome such feelings if work in this field is to progress. We have seen the results of intellectual fossilization in the writings of the Sharp school and the products of the Folklore Society and they are not pretty to look at. The sincerest tribute we can pay to A.L. Lloyd is to continue to work in the critical tradition he has bequeathed us.

*This paper was given at the 'A.L. Lloyd Memorial Conference', London, 4 February 1984.

This paper therefore attempts to look critically at some important aspects of Lloyd's writings both in terms of rejecting what I now feel is unacceptable and affirming those parts which are valuable.

Lloyd's talents formed a rare combination. He was a writer of enormous power; perhaps his talent in this area was developed during his experience as a journalist and scriptwriter. He was also the rare combination of scholar and entertainer. He wore his scholarship lightly but it was none the less real for that. Inevitably he paid the price of people talented in a number of directions in that a real tension existed between the different facets of his public work. This point came over well in Dave Arthur's radio biography[6] and it is clear that Lloyd was aware of it himself towards the end of his life. His unashamed love of the material made him a reassembler and tinkerer with items he came across. There is nothing, in my view wrong with this, but when it is combined with relatively poor documentation, Lloyd lays himself open to the barbs of his critics. Similarly, and of central importance to this paper, I want to argue that his value judgements about the material he dealt with seriously impinged on his work as a social and cultural historian.

Before I develop this theme I want to say something about the central influences on Lloyd's work or to put it in jargon something of the discourses that construct his discourse. In a way not dissimilar to the unusual combination of scholar and entertainer, Lloyd brought an interesting and unique set of influences together in his approach to English folk song. It is worth briefly recapitulating what those influences were, and how they joined together to create his intellectual project.

Let me deal first with Lloyd's political outlook. He was a member of the Communist Party over a long period of time. Most significantly his outlook was formed in the particular period of the 1930s. It was not the classic texts of Marx, Engles, and Lenin that were centrally important to his development, for truly these were not that easily come by at this time.[7] Rather it was the ethos and writings of communist and left intellectuals coupled with the direct experience of unemployment and the workings of the capitalist system that were crucial. If one book is to be singled out for its critical importance I think it must be A.L. Morton's *A People's History of England* first published in a Left Book Club edition in 1938.[8] Morton's book had a great influence on the left in

England, providing a total view of English history from a marxist perspective.

Unlike a great number of those associated with the Historians' Group of the Communist Party, Lloyd (along with Morton and such eminent historians as Eric Hobsbawm) stayed with the Party after the Hungarian Uprising of 1956.[9] I remember seeing Lloyd and Morton share a platform at a meeting of the Historians' Group sometime in the early 1960s. I have a vivid memory of the obvious delight the two men took in each other's company and in the sharing and exchanging of ideas.

If Morton was an important influence on Lloyd so was a historian who did leave the Communist Party in 1956. E.P. Thompson's *The Making of the English Working Class* is quoted in crucial passages in *Folk Song in England*. Whatever the political differences between them, the power of Thompson's great work and its closeness to Lloyd's interests and enthusiasms made it an obvious quarry for Lloyd. The footnoting of the book (which is by the most generous estimate poor) gives no indication of the extent of Lloyd's debt to Thompson. No individual can labour in too many vineyards and Lloyd tended to restrict his work on primary source material to folk song and broadside ballad collections.

An influence that was of profound importance to both Thompson and Lloyd, were the pioneer writings of the radical liberal historians J.L. and Barbara Hammond. Clearly Lloyd had read the Hammonds before writing *The Singing Englishman* in the 1940s.[10] *The Village Labourer*, first published in 1911, gives a stark account of changes in the English countryside in the eighteenth and nineteenth centuries. In recent years it has been savagely attacked by right wing historians and defenders of the agricultural revolution. In some respects the Hammonds' book is overdrawn; for example in the emphasis it places on enclosure of land as the major cause of the impoverishment of the English rural poor. Yet in other ways the book in no way exaggerates the brutal story it has to tell. Its influence on Lloyd was profound, as I hope to show in this paper.

When considering a major historical change such as that which happened in English rural society around the turn of the nineteenth century it is easy to fall into the trap of exaggerating how things were before the change occurred. Relative differences tend to get changed into absolute differences. Even the Hammonds warned against the tendency 'to paint this age as an age of gold'. They reminded their readers that the eighteenth century lived under the shadow of the parson and the squire, that there were disputes between farmers and cottagers but that the system did provide 'opportunities for the humblest and poorest labourer to rise in the village';

> whatever the pressure outside and whatever the bickerings within, it remains true that the common-field system formed a world in which the villagers lived their own lives and cultivated the soil on a basis of independence.[11]

Now listen to Lloyd writing about the same period:

> For at least half the 18th century, life was pretty, plump and easy. There were few embarrasingly rich and few distressingly poor... The stability and equilibrium and relative comfort was felt among the agricutltural labourers too, and how could it be otherwise... there was little crime in the country districts in the first half of the 18th century.[12]

These quotes are lumped together from *The Singing Englishman*. By the time he wrote *Folk Song in England* Lloyd had become a little more guarded in his comments about the eighteenth century, even so he could still write that a labourer living at the time of the Napoleonic Wars 'got to know more about poverty, starvation and crime than his father had ever dreamed of'.[13] He makes what I think is quite a vital error when he writes

> The casual day-labourer without land or common rights was rare enough at this time, though he was soon to become familiar enough.[14]

I want to return to these themes later in this paper but I think I have said enough to show Lloyd's debt to a tradition of radical historiography and I want to say something of the other significant intellectual traditions that went into the making of his thought.

Lloyd's achievement was to place folksong scholarship in England within this tradition of radical history writing. This was by no means a small achievement. Up to this time most writing on traditional music and song had been singularly ahistorical in its nature at least in this country. I think we can trace at least three traditions of folk music scholarship that helped form Lloyd's outlook. Of these the work of Cecil Sharp was, because of Lloyd's central subject, the most important. The work of Sharp and other early collectors has been subject to a considerable amount of critical comment recently.[15] It is not fair to say, as Dave Harker did recently, that Lloyd swallowed most of Sharp whole. It was precisely in the area of historical causation that Lloyd parted company with Sharp. Listen to a paragraph from *The Singing Englishman*:

> Some say the railways killed English folksongs. Some say it was education; some say the industrial revolution. And others, this is God's truth, say the folk songs were 'not altered by environment, but by a fundamental change in the outlook of the people themselves, arising from the attainment of a particular stage in their development' (Cecil Sharp: *English Folksong, Some Conclusions*). How, you may well ask, do people reach a stage in development, without a change in circumstances? How does their outlook alter, except as their social environment alters? The experts are dumb. Perhaps they think these changes just come over people for no special reason like a flock of pigeons off the top of Nelson's cocked hat.[16]

We might justifiably argue that Lloyd's thought is a bit too deterministic here but it would be impossible to argue that this represents the wholesale swallowing of Sharp. What then did Lloyd take from Sharp? Centrally some of his key attitudes and assumptions and, most important, most of his definition of what constitutes folk song. I do not wish to rehearse the arguments of such writers as Harker, Green, and myself on the attitudes, assumptions, and practices of the early folksong collectors in England.[17] Suffice it to say that the concept of folk song embodied in language does not exist in English before the last third of the nineteenth century and that it is essentially a selective category. Its user takes little interest in the actual practice of his or her informants, merely wishing to take from them those items which correspond to the collector's preformed notion of what constitutes the genuine article. It is thus a profoundly ahistorical category, concerned more with aesthetic distinctions made by the collector than with the aesthetic choices made by the performer. The central problem with Lloyd's project as I see it was to attempt to synthesise two traditions which were actually incompatible: radical history and folksong scholarship, the one concerned with an experiential account of the history of the lower classes, the other with an appropriation from lower class culture made to satisfy the romantic feelings of a middle class fraction around the turn of the century. The project was doomed to failure, but it was a magnificent failure and one from which we can learn a vast amount.

But there was more to Lloyd than radical history and Sharpian folksong scholarship and it is important that we recognise these other influences in the making of Lloyd's approach. The most important of these was European and particularly Eastern European folk music scholarship. Here Lloyd's strengths as a linguist payed great dividends and it is here that I must confess my greatest area of uncertainty. When talking to Lloyd it often seemed to me that he would sidestep issues in argument by quoting Eastern European evidence, or if not sidestep issues simply amaze one with the breadth and depth of his learning. Let me quote part of a letter he wrote to me in 1981 to demonstrate what I mean. I had sent him a copy of my article on the collectors in Sussex and Surrey before the First World War. He particularly picked up on the parts that dealt with the problems of singer/collector relationships. Here is a substantial piece of Lloyd in full flow:

> The matter is very complex and, for instance, singers' inhibitions over wide areas of history by no means depend on social difference between tradition-bearer and enquirer. Thus, for instance, I remember Kodaly telling me how much more difficult Bartok found it to collect folk song among Hungarians than Romanians, though the social gap was much wider with the latter. It was just that the Romanians were more outgoing, even to the foreigner, than were the Hungarian peasants, who are indeed a dour lot. As for collecting in Slovak villages, it was just a romp. One singer alone, a Mrs Zuzana Spisjakava, of Poniky in Central Slovakia, gave him 507 songs, in three different visits of 3-4 days each. She sang with utmost willingness, though Bartok remarks: 'She would not at any price sing me songs with indecent texts, though she knew many.' It's rare that the folk show such prudery. Even the Hungarians and still more the Slovaks sing a vast number of such songs and it's particularly the women are the most eager to offer them'. (Vance Randolph found this in the Ozarks. The majority of his dirty stories and songs in the celebrated Bloomington archive of erotic folklore came from women).
>
> Even so, most East European collectors find contact with peasants easier (no barriers, in fact) since 1950 than formerly, though in some areas—Hungary for example, the tide of old-style folk song has much receded in favour of public performance manners.
>
> The problems are innumerable, but your essay is an excellent introduction. In a way, England may be a special case, but they're *all* special cases—none of them alike, as far as variations between 'informant' (hateful word) and folklorist are concerned.[18]

This is not polished writing for publication but those who knew the man will hear the voice behind the words. Yet we must notice certain things about Lloyd's response. In the first place we note the way in which Lloyd immediately springs to Eastern Europe for evidence to flesh out his reply. There is a moment in *Folk Song in England* when Lloyd actually apologises and justifies the use of such evidence:

> Must I apologise for taking examples from such faraway parts? Well-preserved and flourishing traditions yield clearer illustration than traditions in a state of dilapidation like so many in the West.[19]

There is a problem here. The well-preserved and flourishing traditions of Eastern Europe 'yield clearer illustration' than the dilapidated traditions of the West. But can we use this evidence to any great effect if 'they're all special cases' that is if each tradition is the product of a specific set of social and cultural relationships and a specific history. England is a special case, so is Hungary, Romania, the Ozarks, and Sussex. There may be vast areas of similarity yet there will always be differences. Please do not misinterpret me—comparative studies can be of enormous value particularly in the generation of questions and hypotheses, but one cannot simply illustrate one tradition from another. E.P. Thompson has put the point succinctly: 'History knows no regular verbs'.[20]

I must admit a feeling of great ignorance when confronted with Lloyd's material from East European sources. I do not know much of the material and have not the linguistic facility to gain entry to it. Yet I have the strong suspicion that Lloyd used his Balkan evidence selectively. Consider the case of Constantin Brăiloiu (who has too many vowels in his name for the good of any mere English speaker). Clearly Lloyd knew his work, he refers to him in *Folk Song in England*, as raising and sidestepping the issue of what we are to understand by 'folk', is credited with the idea that a song really only exists at the moment of performance, is quoted on the subject of disputed authorship in Romanian villages, is allowed to comment on Bartók and Kodaly's analysis and characterisation of the melody of Hungarian folk song, is given as a source for a quote from Georges Sand on Berrichon bagpipe music, and is credited with refinement in the techniques of notating folk tunes along with Bartók.[21] Here is an important source for Lloyd's thought yet there is a vital absence. Lloyd discusses in great detail the nature of folk song and yet never discusses Brăiloiu's early and formidable critique of the way collectors pre-selected their material contrasted with the way collectors ought to have worked if they were being scientific.[22] This is the same area of discussion that Lloyd failed to pick up on when commenting on my folksong collectors essay.[23] It is a very significant question why Lloyd found this area so difficult and perhaps painful to discuss. The only answer can be that he so shared the Sharpian notion that folk song existed as a pure category that questions like this were ruled out of order. To Lloyd a folk song was something that had particular qualities, it could be distinguished by comparison with that which was not a folk song which did not have these qualities. He certainly held a notion of the deterioration of tradition, the urban songs of the 1820s and after being described as a 'miserable and undistinguished sort of thing' compared with what had been produced before.[24]

I started this paper trying to note some of the important elements that went into the making of Lloyd's approach. Along the way I have made some digressions to suggest the actual uses he made of these elements and some of the problems associated with such uses. I want to conclude this part of the paper by noting two other important influences before looking in detail at his theory of historical and musical change.

As well as European folk music scholarship, American work in this area was an important, if somewhat less important influence. In some ways this is a more obvious source for a student of English folk song than to go to the Balkans, but Lloyd rarely went for the obvious. Nevertheless the work of such people as Vance Randolph, Phillips Barry, Samuel Bayard, and George Korson did have an influence.[25] Alan Lomax's *magnum opus* on 'cantometrics' *Folk Song Style and Culture* was published the year after *Folk Song in England* but Lomax's idea of linking singing style with the type of society had had a good airing in article form before the publication of the book.[26] Lloyd nowhere alludes to this thesis in his work. I remember having dinner with Lloyd in about 1973 when I, as an enthusiastic mature under-graduate seeking an easy answer to the problem of the universe, was very impressed with Lomax's book. He would not be drawn on the subject restricting his comment to a contemptuous 'Alan is a good journalist'. With hindsight and experience I can now see what he was getting at.

The last influence I want to refer to in the making of Lloyd's outlook is the influence of the discipline of folklore. Unlike some recent writers

Lloyd never shied away from using this term because of its antiquarian and fossilized connotations. On the contrary Lloyd was rather keen on such phrases as 'musical folklore' and 'folklore science'. The essence of the study of folklore as it developed in nineteenth century England was the search for 'primitive survivals' in social practices and cultural artifacts. Folklore foregrounded one aspect, in my view a very unimportant aspect and often non-verifiable one of practices and artifacts. It engaged on a barren quest for origins, a word that had almost mystical significance in the folklorist's vocabulary, marginalising important questions about the meaning, significance, and function of the custom or item of repertory. Folklore is not interested in historical questions other than the unanswerable question about ultimate origins. As Bourdieu has written 'explanation in terms of survival explains nothing unless one can explain why the survival survives'.[27]

This type of folklore had a subtle and pervasive effect on Lloyd's writing. Certainly he handled this aspect of his work in a more sensible way than a large numbr of recent writers stuck in the time warp of this tradition. But the mental set is still there in Lloyd and I have the feeling (prejudice perhaps) that it works against his real qualities as a historian. People must decide this for themselves and I would suggest that they reread the chapter on 'The Big Ballads', the section on erotic song, and the comment on 'The Saucy Bold Robber' that 'The tatters of some bygone epic hero still seem to flutter round the shoulders of that plucky sailor'. The problem with folklorism is that it tends to make us think in terms of degeneration, decay, and fragmentation, rather than in terms of change.

These then are the intellectual traditions from which Lloyd made his remarkable synthesis: radical history, the folksong scholarship of England, Europe (notably the Balkans) and the USA, and the tradition of folklore scholarship both in its quasi-mystical English variety and its somewhat more scientific variety as practised in Eastern Europe. I want to now try to see how Lloyd combined these traditions and melded them into a theory of musical and historical change.

Lloyd introduces his theory—perhaps hypothesis is a better term—in a persuasive and subtle way in *Folk Song in England*. Early on in the first 'foundations' chapter[28] he floats the idea that a tradition may, as the result of slow, almost imperceptible, changes building up, suddenly be radically changed in a fairly dramatic way.

A song may be born into a tradition that fits a certain society; but as that society changes, as the folk change, the song may change too. A folk song tradition is not a fixed and immutable affair, and the word 'authenticity', favourite among amateurs of folk music, is one to be used with caution. Traditionalists are always disturbed by the appearance of novelties on the folkloric scene, but in any living tradition novelties are constantly emerging, often in tiny almost imperceptible details that accumulate over long periods of time and suddenly, when the social moment is ripe, come together to result in a change that may be drastic.

Those with an ear for such things will hear behind this passage a loud echo of 'the law of the transformation of quality into quantity and vice versa' a cornerstone of marxist philosophy, little discussed in recent years but seemingly of great importance to English communists of earlier generations.[29] The notion is used both in an explanatory way and in a predictive way, as an explanation for historical events and as a justification for the growth and development of a revolutionary party. The scientificity of the notion was assured by an appeal to the 'dialectics of nature', but the law was said equally to apply to human society.

> The social revolution itself is just such a 'jump', where accumulated quantitative alterations pass into qualitative change.[30]

If all social phenomena are subject to this law, why then should folk song be exempt from it?

Lloyd then proceeds to give 'a dramatic illustration of this process'. Those who heard Lloyd lecture will be familiar with the story of the Romanian folklorists who revisited an area in which Bartók had collected forty years previously. A wonderful transformation had taken place. In place of the 'limited, even primitive' songs of Bartók's day, middle-aged performers now gave 'grand, spacious, flowery, meandering, rather dreamy and reflective' songs. Younger singers gave many newly made songs 'little-ornamented, four-square in shape, rather wide in compass, of great rhythmic impetuosity, sung in excited energetic fashion... and generally with an optimistic air'. What accounted for this change? Expansion of the rural economy and improvement in transportation between the wars with subsequent increase in cultural contact

> and the change was intensified and given a new direction with the establishing of the Communist government after the Second World

War when the young villagers in particular became filled with a sense of purpose that their parents had often lacked, passivity was replaced with initiative, apathy by elation, humility by a sense of self importance.[31]

The local song tradition was robust enough to respond to new material perspectives and widening cultural horizons.

Let us take stock of what Lloyd had documented here, for it is the mirror image of what will come later. Cultural change, the enlivening of the dour singing tradition is linked to economic and political change. This is no mere theorising around the marxist notion of economic base and cultural superstructure, but an empirically verifiable, well documented case of inter-related musical and historical change. The sources are impeccable, if somewhat inaccessable to the Western reader. The sceptic however might raise a question mark over the way in which Bartók selected his material, and whether the Romanian folklorists (good comrades all no doubt) set out, perhaps subconsciously, to demonstrate the positive cultural response of the peasantry to socialism. We will leave the matter there, as I do not have access to the sources to allow me to investigate my reservations.

Lloyd returns to the subject of historical and musical change at the start of the fourth chapter of *Folk Song in England*, 'The Lyrical Songs and Later Ballads',[32] with a gesture towards Indian elephant drivers in African logging districts and Transylvanian villages he begins to discuss the rise of the English middle class after 1500 and its affect on the music of village green and kitchen.

> Nor need we be surprised that, at a later date, with great change overtaking the life of many country workers towards the end of the eighteenth century, the folk tradition took one of those famous qualitative leaps and, within a dramatically short time (it seems) the songs presented a new face in which some of the old features were recognizable but the expression was much altered.[33]

In summary form Lloyd's thesis is that 'while English folk song is unitary, two stages are none the less perceptible'. The key moment of change is the second half of the eighteenth century, the period when according to the Hammonds, English rural society was transformed by enclosure.

Lloyd characterises the 'early tradition' and 'late tradition' in this way:

In general the earlier melodies are more vigorous, squarer, franker in cast, their harmonic structure dominated by the common chord. The newer versions tend rather to be dominated by the fourth, their rhythm is elastic, they incline to hover and take unexpected directions; their formal structure is well-enough defined but their intonations may be so surprising as to baffle the unaccustomed listener.[34]

Two major problems with this passage suggest themselves to me. One is to do with evidence the other is to do with Lloyd's characterisation of the late tradition.

Lloyd's evidence for the bluff early tradition is tunes recorded before 1750 and accessible to us in the collections of Chappell and Simpson.[35] Lloyd realises that he may be building a house on sand. He quotes Sharp to the effect that we cannot accept as genuine folk products tunes printed in the eighteenth century and earlier *without discrimination*. 'Neither should we, without discrimination push them aside.' Lloyd's view is that we can use such material as evidence on matters like characteristic tune shape. This seems to me a clear case of having your cake and eating it. One cannot on the one hand set up a case for the uniqueness of folk music, for its difference from what has come down to us from the written records, for its orality and malleability and at the same time hope that the chance survivals of written tunes from earlier centuries—centuries before the notion of scientific collecting existed— will tell us a great deal about it. Obviously there is a relationship between surviving tunes and what was popularly performed—'Packington's Pound', 'Greensleeves', and 'Fortune my Foe' were popularly and probably widely performed. But *how* were they performed? That which looks vigorous or square and frank in cast and dominated by the structure of the common chord may not have sounded like that in performance. And what is absent from the written record? Think what we would never have had if Sharp and his eccentric contemporaries had not done their work.

Equally we must ask whether Lloyd's characterisation of the late tradition is reasonable, those hovering tunes which take unexpected directions and baffle the unaccustomed listener. Certainly Lloyd loved tunes of this sort but are they characteristic of the tradition of the whole? I will return to this point later.

Let us again take stock of what Lloyd has thus far accomplished. He has shown us that a relationship exists between song, economics, and politics in twentieth century Transylvania. He has argued that English folk song exists in two stages, a confident earlier tradition and a hesitant later tradition. He has stated that this bifurcated tradition is in someway related to the rise of the middle class but he has not as yet made any tangible connections. It is important to summarise how Lloyd's argument proceeds as his method is very persuasive. He builds his argument in layers and allows the reader time to absorb one layer before he adds the next. But there may also be an element of reification in his method, for what is tentative and suggested in one layer may be treated as hard fact in the next. Thus the 'sudden qualitative leap' in Transylvanian singing style becomes 'One of those famous qualitative leaps' in chapter four and the hypothesis that two stages in the creation of English folk songs are perceptible becomes 'an increasing number of melodies were being created in a different shape and spirit, in the more circuitous tentative manner of the "newer tradition"' by the time Lloyd picks up this theme again fifty or so pages later.

Seeming to have now established that such a change did take place, Lloyd boldly asks the question, 'Why should English folk melody, in part at least, so change its nature?'. The discrepancies cannot be explained away on the grounds of editorial interference. He dismisses the notion of English acculturation of Irish singing styles in little over a page.

> If indeed the style was affected by models brought in by Irish labourers, what psychological factors disposed the English singers to adopt these enchanting hesitancies, these hovering mysteries that pervade so much of our countryside lyric as the later collectors found it?[36]

That 'as the later collectors found it' is very telling. Maybe the qualities that Lloyd is interpreting as being characteristic of the later tradition are precisely those characteristics that the Victorian and Edwardian collectors took such delight in. Perhaps they selected songs with these characteristics from the wider repertories of the rural singers. Thus Lloyd's vision of change may be a myopic vision based on unreliable data.

Lloyd's thesis is that it was the folksinging part of the community that was most affected by enclosure and rationalised farming. That their psychological response to misfortune caused them to favour 'a looser, vaguer, less sure and confident style of melody'. This is the musical history the Hammonds never wrote, the complement to their great work. It is a wonderful theory but I feel it won't bear the weight of historical criticism. Where can we hear this style of singing and melody? In the recordings made by the collectors before 1914? I cannot hear it there, the great Joseph Taylor's singing, decorated and surprising as it is, is never loose, vague, unsure, or unconfident. Much of the repertory of traditional singers recorded in the last eighty years seems firmly set in Lloyd's earlier tradition, the singing is confident, the tunes are four-square and based upon the common chord and there seems little of hesitancy or vagueness. I cite as my evidence numerous singers recorded this century. Certainly there are differences in style and presentation, for example between the stoicism of Harry Cox and the exuberance of Sam Larner, but I do not hear the qualities Lloyd writes of overmuch except in one place: the singing of A.L. Lloyd himself. Our musical practice is always a synthesis of our musical experiences and the ideas we have about music. To Lloyd certain characteristics in English traditional song had significance beyond their intrinsic qualities, they told the story of the demise of the English peasantry, the class robbery of enclosure, the destruction of the conditions under which English rural folk song flourished. The study of music as a sign system, musical semiotics, is in its infancy. It is instructive that one of its early lessons is that any musical characteristic or set of characteristics can have vastly different significances for different hearers. We do not all hear what Lloyd heard in English folk song.

I have argued earlier in this paper that Lloyd's project was doomed to failure. My reason for holding this view is that two of the traditions he drew on, radical history and Sharpian folksong scholarship, are in the last analysis, not able to be synthesised. There are too many elements within each of these traditions that jar and rub against each other for them to rest happily within the same covers. The one is a romantic, middle-class ideology from the turn of the century essentially unself-critical and conservative in its outlook, the other, romantic and middle class as it sometimes seems, is nevertheless through the practice of historical criticism, essentially critical and radical. The former is a working out of a preconceived aesthetic outlook, the latter through the interaction of theory and empirical research is always both destroying and renewing itself.

In some ways this has been a rather negative paper; I have attempted a brief deconstruction of a central aspect of Lloyd's work and this is the second paper I have devoted to doing so. I do not wish to end on a negative note and I do wish to say something more about why I have devoted my time and energy to these projects.

To me, *Folk Song in England* is the most important book I have ever read. As my battered paperback copy will testify, for years I have read it, derived pleasure from it, sung from it, worried about it, silently and recently not so silently argued with it. In many ways it has played a large part in shaping my life. It was central in stimulating my interest in history which led me to go to university and take a degree. The whole of my subsequent research work has in a sense been a critical engagement with Lloyd, and this is overwhelmingly a positive response to his work. Lloyd was the pioneer, he gave us a map and asked a great number of the right questions, but he built on what was available to him; the book has the strengths and weaknesses of a pioneer work.

Folk Song in England is getting on for twenty years old, the thinking in it is older than the publication date. How different would the book have been if Lloyd had finished it last year or undertaken a thorough revision of it? This is speculation but I feel Lloyd might well have taken on board some of the subsequent criticism and discussion in the field.

Lloyd intended to reply to my 'Song, Sex and Society' article but death intervened. The article argued strongly against Lloyd's romantic interpretation of traditional erotic song. In the piece I argued that Lloyd's view that the songs represented a clean and joyful acceptance of sexuality was not tenable in the light of historical criticism. The nearest thing we have to the response Lloyd would have made are the comments on the piece he sent to the editor of the *Folk Music Journal*. I think they are worth publishing as they stand.

> Certainly worth publishing. If it is published, might I be allowed to make a couple of tail-piece comments? On the question of the myth of the uninhibited peasant: over the years since *Folk Song in England* was published I have modified some of my views. Nowadays I would agree that as 'spokesman' for the myth I wrote far too lyrically.
>
> On the matter of the downright obscene song (or pornographic song) and my 'hatred of such pieces', I was thinking rather of the kind of loveless and cruel songs such as we find in, say, the rugger club repertory (such as *The Fucking Machine* or *The Big Wheel*). I recognise that my view was subjective, without any basis in folklore science. I was affected partly by the fact that so much material of the kind gives the impression of being created by a different social class from the one that we habitually regard as the makers (or evolvers) of traditional song. Nowadays I recognise that the creation of folklore is

not so restricted. The inhabitants of the 'paper empire'—clerks, actors, professional people etc., have their own fund of anecdote, legend, superstition and such, even if they don't as a rule run to the making of songs, in the manner of boisterous companies such as the rugger clubs. So I suppose it's incorrect to relegate such creations to 'the margin of tradition'. (Subjectively, I've still no fancy for scatological or sadistic songs; however sexy, I prefer a bit of fondness, but that's a private view).[37]

Here we have it, Lloyd was willing to modify his views and he was able to see some of the subjectivity that went into his own writing. We are all entitled to our subjectivity, although we owe it to our readers to try and become self-conscious of it and disentangle the fact and value in our work. Here is some subjectivity. I will remember A.L. Lloyd with more than a bit of fondness. That's a private view but one I think shared by many people.

NOTES

In spite of the lapse of time between the delivery of this paper at the 'A.L. Lloyd Memorial Conference' and its subsequent publication I have chosen not to revise the text. My thoughts and feelings about Lloyd remain substantially the same as expressed in the text although errors and subsequent developments are detailed in these notes.

1. Maud Karpeles, *An Introduction to English Folk Song* (London; Oxford University Press, 1973). Frank Howes, *Folk Music of Britain—and Beyond* (London: Hutchinson, 1969).

2. I have spoken to two people about this work, Reg Hall and Douggie Moncrieff, both of whom spoke very highly of it. Is it too much to hope that the work of this undoubted pioneer might yet be made available to a wider readership?

3. In some ways the use of different methods, for example detailed historical research or participant observation, can be read as an implicit expression of dissatisfaction with Lloyd's work. Informal criticism of his work, expressing itself in comments and in different modes of musical practice, has been widespread since the 1960s.

4. Dave Harker, 'Bert Lloyd', paper given at the conference 'New Perspectives on Traditional Music', Cecil Sharp House, 26 February 1983. A later version was given at the International Association for the Study of Popular Music conference at Reggio Emilia, Italy, September 1983 and will be published in the conference proceedings. This material has now been published in Harker's book

Fakesong: The Manufacture of British 'Folksong' 1700 to the Present Day (Milton Keynes: Open University Press, 1985). For a critique of Harker's approach see Vic Gammon, 'Two for the Show: David Harker, Politics and Popular Song', *History Workshop*, 21 (Spring 1986).

5. Vic Gammon, 'Song, Sex and Society in England, 1600-1850', *Folk Music Journal*, 4 (1982), 208-45.

6. Dave Arthur, '"As I roved out": A Life of A.L. Lloyd', BBC Radio 4, broadcast Saturday 1 October 1983. Arthur presented a fascinating and delightful biographical paper at this conference. The anticipated book on Lloyd's life is something to look forward to.

7. See Eric Hobsbawm, 'The Historians' Group of the Communist Party', in *Rebels and their Causes: Essays in Honour of A.L. Morton*, edited by Maurice Cornforth (London: Lawrence and Wishart, 1978) and Raphael Samuel, 'British Marxist Historians, 1880-1980: Part One', *New Left Review*, 120 (March-April 1980). Both these essays give interesting perspectives on the background of left intellectuals at this period.

8. A.L. Morton, *A People's History of England* (London: Victor Gollancz, 1938).

9. Hobsbawm, pp. 39-40.

10. A.L. Lloyd, *The Singing Englishman* (London: Workers' Music Association, no date), pp. 40-51.

11. J.L. Hammond and Barbara Hammond, *The Village Labourer* (London: Longman, 1978), p. 6.

12. Lloyd, *Englishman*, pp. 36 and 42.

13. A.L. Lloyd, *Folk Song in England* (London: Lawrence and Wishart, 1967), p. 234; the paperback edition (London: Panther, 1969), p. 236, is referred to throughout this paper.

14. Lloyd, *Folk Song in England*, p. 230.

15. David Harker, 'Cecil Sharp in Somerset: Some Conclusions', *Folk Music Journal*, 2 (1972), 220-40; Dave Harker, 'May Cecil Sharp Be Praised?' *History Workshop Journal*, 14 (1982), 44-62; Vic Gammon, 'Folk Song Collecting in Sussex and Surrey, 1843-1914', *History Workshop Journal*, 10 (1980), 61-89; Dave Harker, *Fakesong*, generally.

16. Lloyd, *Englishman*, p. 52.

17. See note 15.

18. A.L. Lloyd to Vic Gammon, 20 February 1981.

19. Lloyd, *Folk Song in England*, p. 72.

20. E.P. Thompson, *The Poverty of Theory* (London: Merlin Press, 1978), p. 238.

21. Lloyd, *Folk Song in England*, pp. 22, 25, 50, 68, 413, 414. Since this was written, A.L. Lloyd's translations of important essays by Constantin Brăiliou have been published as *Problems of Ethnomusicology* (Cambridge: Cambridge

University Press, 1984). I feel that my ignorance led me to overstress the potential influence of Brăiloiu's 'scientific' method. As Brăiliou's writings show, Lloyd's debt to him was considerable but at the same time the two men had much in common. Both were, in a sense, deeply romantic and backward looking. See my review of the Brăiliou book in *Folk Music Journal*, 5 (1985), 107-109.

22. Brăiliou, *Problems*, generally but particularly 1 to 101.

23. A.L. Lloyd to Vic Gammon, 20 February 1981.

24. Lloyd, *Englishman*, p. 48.

25. Lloyd, *Folk Song in England*, pp. 103, 20, 62, 83, 232, 386, 388.

26. Alan Lomax, *Folk Song Style and Culture* (Washington: American Association for the Advancement of Science, 1968).

27. Pierre Bourdieu and Jean-Claude Passeron, *Reproduction in Education, Society and Culture* (London: Sage Publications, 1977), p. 149.

28. Lloyd, *Folk Song in England*, p. 72.

29. See Samuel, 'British Marxist Historians'.

30. David Guest, *Lectures on Marxist Philosophy* (London: Lawrence and Wishart, 1963) first published as *A Textbook of Dialectical Materialism* (1939), p. 39.

31. Lloyd, *Folk Song in England*, p. 74.

32. Lloyd, *Folk Song in England*, pp. 173-75.

33. Lloyd, *Folk Song in England*, pp. 173 and 175.

34. Lloyd, *Folk Song in England*, p. 174.

35. Lloyd, *Folk Song in England*, pp. 174 and 175. William Chappell, *Popular Music of the Olden Time* (London: Chappell, 1859), reprinted edition (New York: Dover, 1965). Claude Simpson, *The British Broadside Ballad and its Music* (New Brunswick, N.J.: Rutgers University Press, 1966).

36. Lloyd, *Folk Song in England*, p. 233.

37. A.L. Lloyd to Ian Russell, 23 November 1981.

A.L. LLOYD 1908-82: AN INTERIM BIBLIOGRAPHY*

David Arthur

For the last three years I have been collecting material for a biography of Bert Lloyd: this interim bibliography is a by-product of the research to date. It is presented in the full knowledge of its omissions and shortcomings, but in the hope that it might encourage someone to blow the dust from some old magazines and help me to fill in the gaps. Despite its incompleteness I would like to think that this first A.L. Lloyd bibliography contains enough interesting material to provide a fairly accurate picture of Bert's literary outpourings over fifty years.

An important area of Bert's writing that falls outside the scope of this present offering is his work for radio and television. Between 1938 and his death in 1982 he wrote over 150 radio scripts and some half-dozen television films. Apart from such classic music programmes as *Songs of the Durham Miners* (1963), *The Folk Song Virtuoso* (1966), *The Voice of the Gods* (1967), and *The Origins of Polyphony* (1968), the majority of his radio writing was undertaken for the BBC Schools Department. The scripts, many of them drama-documentaries, covered a bewildering range of subjects from the 'Common Cold' to the 'Lives of Patagonian Shepherds'. A number of them were autobiographical and give us some interesting glimpses of little known aspects of his life such as his time on the sheep stations of New South Wales (*A Bush Fire in Australia*); his trip to the South Atlantic on the factory-ship Southern Empress

*I would like to thank the following people for their help and encouragement in the compilation of this bibliography: Kenneth Bell, James Cameron, Vic Gammon, Bert Hardy, Dave Harker, Sir Tom Hopkinson, Alun Howkins, Sir Edward Hulton, Lawrence and Wishart Ltd., A.L. Morton, Paul Oliver, Michael Pickering, Camilla Raab, Vic Smith, Malcolm Taylor, Michael and Betty Wippell, and, of course, Charlotte Lloyd. Any additions will be gratefully received as will any comments, views, or information on Bert Lloyd's life and work. Please write to 3 Forge Cottages, Boats Head, Crowborough, East Sussex, TN6 3HD.

(*Whaling in the Antarctic*) and even his experiences as a one-eyed shantyman in John Huston's *Moby Dick* (*Film Extra at Sea*).

With the help of his German born wife, Charlotte, he also translated numerous plays for the BBC's Drama Department. These included, Brecht's *St Joan of the Stockyards* and *Mother Courage and her Children*, which Brecht considered 'a rather good translation'.

His television writing came late in life and then more by accident than design. A Greenwich neighbour was a BBC television editor named Norman Swallow and, in 1970 when director Barrie Gavin was thinking of making an *Omnibus* film about British folk music, Swallow recommended that he should get in touch with Bert Lloyd. The subsequent, fortuitous, meeting resulted in the widely acclaimed television film *Rap her to Bank*, a study of the life and music of the mining community of the North-East.

More Gavin/Lloyd collaborations followed over the next ten years, taking the pair of them from Padstow to Rumania, and from the Hebrides to the Appalachians. Bert's earlier journalistic training paid dividends when it came to writing film scripts; he could always be relied upon to come up with an apposite, pithy, poetic, or amusing film link, no matter how seemingly disparate the shots—and always timed to the second.

Bert also tackled reviewing: in the 1930s he reviewed novels for *Left Review*; biography and kitchen design(!) for the weekly paper *Reynolds News* and from 1956 up to the 1980s he regularly contributed to the *Journal of the EFDSS* and its continuation, the *Folk Music Journal*. At editorial board meetings of the *Folk Music Journal* anything published in Russian, German, Rumanian, and half-a-dozen other languages, naturally gravitated to Bert's end of the table; he would pick it up, flick through it and say: 'Oh yes, I think I can do something with this'.

Then there were the countless sleeve notes that he contributed to Topic Records during his several years' reign as the company's Artistic Director. Informative and succinct, they were models of erudition that set the standard for all subsequent folkmusic album notes.

Although his marxist beliefs obviously imposed a strong political bias upon Bert's interpretation and presentation of facts and events, he was, at the same time, a stickler for exactitude over minor details such as the spelling of a name or a book title: he once took me to task for not hyphenating 'Folk Songs' in the title of Alfred Williams' *Folk-Songs of the Upper Thames*.

In later life he regretted his earlier somewhat cavalier attitude to scholarship and latterly did his best to make amends. In all fairness, a lot of the things of which Bert has been accused, such as re-writing and fitting new tunes to songs without always making the facts clear, were, I'm sure, the results of his natural artistic creativity and not conscious scholarly skulduggery. For over forty years Bert earned his living by his pen and was still working on and thinking about new schemes right up to his death. Barrie Gavin, who visited Bert just before he died, recounts how Bert, who was very weak and who knew that he was dying said: 'Isn't it a buggar? I've got so many ideas and I can't get them down on paper'. What those ideas were we'll never know, but I think that, unlike Bartók, who said on *his* deathbed that he was leaving with a full suitcase, Bert managed to unpack a fair amount of his literary and musical baggage and hopefully only went off with a shoulder bag.

Books

(Unless otherwise shown, all books were published in London.)

1937   Federico Garcia Lorca, *Lament for the Death of a Bullfighter and other poems* in the original Spanish with English translation by A.L. Lloyd, William Heinemann, 48pp.

1940   *Shadow of the Swastika*, with L. Vinogradoff, Lane, 200pp., 8 ill.

1944   *The Singing Englishman: An Introduction to Folksong*, Keynote Series Book 4, Workers' Music Association, 70 pp., paperbound.

1945   *Corn on the Cob: Popular and Traditional Poetry of the USA*, selected by A.L. Lloyd, Fore Publications, 66pp., paperbound.

c. 1945   *20 songs* for three part accompanied or unaccompanied singing, selected by A.L. Lloyd, arranged by Alan Bush. Workers' Music Association, 28pp., paperbound.

1945   *Twelve Russian Folk Songs for Children*, English texts and notes by A.L. Lloyd. Music arranged by Matyas Seiber, Workers' Music Association, 16pp., paperbound.

1951   *Singing Englishmen: Festival of Britain Song Book*, edited by A.L. Lloyd, Workers' Music Association, 23 songs with music, 44pp., paperbound.

1952   *Come All Ye Bold Miners: Ballads and Songs of the Coalfields*, edited by A.L. Lloyd, Lawrence and Wishart, 16 musical examples, 144pp.

1952   Hans Fallada, pseud. (Rudolph F. Ditzen), *The Drinker*, translated by A.L. and Charlotte Lloyd, Putnam.

1952   *Coaldust Ballads*, compiled by A.L. Lloyd, arrangements by Alan Bush, Will Sahnow, John Miller, Bernard Stevens, Robert Gill, and Matyas Seiber. 20 songs with music, Workers' Music Association, 40pp., paperbound.

1953   Dieter Meichsner, *Vain Glory*, translated by A.L. and Charlotte Lloyd, Putnam, 247pp.

1953   *Lament for the Death of a Bullfighter and other poems*, new edition, Heinemann.

1954   *Dances of Argentina*, Traditional Dances of Latin America Series, Max Parrish, 40pp., 4 col. ill.

1955   Kurt Frieberger, *Simon Peter the Fisherman*, translated by A.L. Lloyd, Heinemann, 372pp.

1956   Ion Creanga (pseud: Ion Stefanescu), *Recollections from Childhood*, translated and foreword by A.L. Lloyd, Library of Rumanian Literature Series, Lawrence and Wishart, 124pp.

1957   *Simon Peter the Fisherman*, re-issue Heinemann.

1959   *The Penguin Book of English Folk Songs*, edited by Ralph Vaughan Williams and A.L. Lloyd, Harmondsworth: Penguin Books, 70 songs with tunes, 128pp., paperbound.

1960   *Vain Glory*, new paperback edition, Panther Books (Hamilton and Company, Stafford Ltd), 192pp.

1960   *The Golden City*, A.L. Lloyd and Pearl Binder, Methuen, 48pp., 13 col. ill.

1960   *Sea Shanties and Songs* (The *Treasure Island* Song Book), adapted and arranged with new lyrics by A.L. Lloyd, from the New Production of *Treasure Island* at the Mermaid Theatre, Keith Prowse, 17pp.

1965   *Folk Songs of the Americas*, A.L. Lloyd and I.A. de R. Rivera, Novello (prepared for the International Folk Music Council), 150 songs with tunes, 276pp.

1967   *Folk Song in England*, Lawrence and Wishart, 433pp., 105 musical examples. Also New York: International Publishers.

1969   *Folk Song in England*, new paperback edition, Panther Books, 448pp.

1975   *Folk Song in England*, new paperback edition, Paladin Books, 416pp.

1978   *Come All Ye Bold Miners*, second revised edition, Lawrence and Wishart, 76 musical examples, 384pp.

1980   Tiberiu Alexandru, *Rumanian Folk Music*, translated by Constantin Stihi-Boos, translation revised by A.L. Lloyd, Bucharest: Musical Publishing House, 269pp.

Constantin Brăiloiu *Ale Mortului: Din Gorj* (Songs 'To the Dead' from Gorj), Societatea Compozitorilor Romani, Publicatiile Archive De Folklore (Bucharest 1936), commentary and translations by A.L. Lloyd, 12pp.

1984   Constantin Brăiloiu, *Problems of Ethnomusicology*, edited and translated by A.L. Lloyd, Cambridge University Press, xix + 299pp.

Articles, Essays, Poems

1934   'The Red Steer' (short story), *The Left Review*, 1, no. 1 (October 1934), 26-30.

1935   'Modern Art and Modern Society', in *5 On Revolutionary Art*, Artists International Association and Martin Lawrence (November 1935), 88pp.

c. 1936   'Lament for Ignacio Sanchez Mejias', Federico Garcia Lorca, translated by A.L. Lloyd, sections in *The Listener*, later published in revised version by William Heinemann, 1937.

c. 1936   'Lament for Ignacio Sanchez Mejias', Federico Garcia Lorca, translated by A.L. Lloyd, sections in *Contemporary Poetry and Prose*.

1937   'The Tragedy of Lorca', *The Listener*, 17, no. 420 (27 January 1937), 184.

1937   'Surrealism and Revolutions', *The Left Review*, 2, no. 16 (January 1937), 895-98. A 'Reply to A.L. Lloyd' by Herbert Read and Hugh Sykes Davies appeared in *The Left Review*, 3, no. 1 (February 1937), 47-48.

1937   *Daily Worker* (10 February 1937). Article on the influence of capitalism on folk-art (see Ian Watson, *Song and Democratic Culture in Britain*, Croom Helm, 1983, p. 35).

c. 1937   *Artists International Association News Sheet*, article attacking Bernard Causton's 'Art in Germany Under the Nazis' (*The Studio* November 1936). (See AIA, *The Story of the Artists International Association 1933-1953*, L. Morris and R. Radford, The Museum of Modern Art, Oxford, 1983, p. 51).

1937   'The Dawn' (poem), Federico Garcia Lorca, translated by A.L. Lloyd, in *New Writing* 4, edited by John Lehmann, Lawrence and Wishart (Autumn 1937), 177.

1937   'The New Spectacle of Wonders: A masquerade in one act' (play), Raphael Dieste, translated from the Spanish by A.L. Lloyd, in *New*

Writing 4, edited by John Lehmann, Lawrence and Wishart (Autumn 1937), 232-244.

1937   'Lorca: Poet of Spain', *The Left Review*, 3, no. 2 (March 1937), 71-74. Includes Lloyd's translation of 'The Faithless Wife' later published in *Lament for the Death of a Bullfighter*, Heinemann, 1937.

1939   'The Winds of the People' (poem), Miguel Hernández (1910-42), translated by A.L. Lloyd, in *Poems for Spain*, edited by John Lehmann and Stephen Spender, Hogarth Press, 1939.

1939   'Shadow of the Swastika', *Reynolds News*, serialised, 28 January, 4, 11, 18, 25 February, 3 March, based on BBC series with new material not broadcast.

1940   'The Story of New Zealand (1840-1940)', *Picture Post*, 6, no. 6 (10 February 1940), 28-36.

1940   'The East End at War', *Picture Post*, 8, no. 13 (28 September 1940), 9-18, photographs by Bert Hardy.

1940   'The Life of an East End Parson', *Picture Post*, 9, no. 8 (23 November 1940), 9-13, photographs by Bert Hardy.

1940   'Christmas is Coming at the Eel's Foot', *Picture Post*, 9, no. 11 (14 December 1940), 22-23, photographs by Bert Hardy.

1941   'Committee in Revolt', *Picture Post*, 12, no. 3 (19 July 1941), 26-27, 30.

1941   'Parish War Cabinet', *Picture Post*, 12, no. 7 (16 August 1941), 22-23.

1941   'The Most Important Lunch Party of the War', *Picture Post*, 12, no. 11 (13 September 1941), 7-9, photographs by Bert Hardy.

1942   'At Sea with the Wartime Trawlermen', *Picture Post*, 14, no. 12 (21 March 1942), 5-10, photographs by Bert Hardy.

1942–   *The Turret*. A weekly left-wing(?) service newspaper produced by Frank Owen (later editor of *Seac*), A.L. Lloyd and others during time in 52nd Training Regiment, Royal Armoured Corps.

1942   'The Cowboy and his Music', *University Forward* (Organ of the University Labour Federation), 7, no. 5 (May 1942), 20-27 (No music); later reprinted in *Our Time* (1943).

1943   'The Cowboy and his Music', *Our Time*, 2, no. 10 (April 1943), 12-20; reprinted from *University Forward* (1942),with new musical examples.

c.1943 'The Revolutionary Origins of English Folk-Song', *William Morris Musical Society Bulletin*; later expanded into *The Singing Englishman* (1944).

c.1943 'The Revolutionary Origins of English Folk-Song', *Folk--review of people's music*, Part 1 (February 1945), 13-15; originally in *William*

Morris Musical Society Bulletin, Workers Music Association (*c*.1943).

1945   'Black Spirituals and White', *Modern Quarterly*, 1, no. 1 (1945), 71-88.

1946   'The Dawn' (poem), Federico Garcia Lorca, translated by A.L. Lloyd, *Poems from New Writing 1936-1946* selected by J. Lehmann, Lehmann, 1946, pp. 22-23.

1946   'The Disney Team at work', *Picture Post*, 30, no. 12 (23 March 1946), 21-23.

1946   'Can German Prisoners Learn Democracy?' *Picture Post*, 31, no. 1 (6 April 1946), 11-13, 29, photographs by K. Hutton.

1946   'Argentina Votes Itself a Dictator', *Picture Post*, 31, no. 4 (27 April 1946), 10-13, 29.

1946   'A Prophet Holds a Revival Meeting', *Picture Post*, 31, no. 6 (11 May 1946), 10-13, 29.

1946   'The Most Popular Girl in Britain', *Picture Post*, 31, no. 12 (22 June 1946), 24-26.

1946   'A New Opera for Glyndebourne', *Picture Post*, 32, no. 2 (13 July 1946), 25-27, photographs by Gerti Deutsch.

1946   'A People Moves out', *Picture Post*, 32, no. 7 (17 August 1946), 15-18, 29, photographs by Raymond Kleboe.

1946   'Czechoslovakia: A Peasant's Life', *Picture Post*, 32, no. 10 (7 September 1946), 21-25, 29, photographs by R. Kleboe.

1946   'The Days of the West', *Transatlantic Quarterly*, no. 35 (Autumn 1946), 10-19.

1946   'Portraits from the King's Collection', *Picture Post*, 33, no. 11 (14 December 1946), 18-20.

1946   'An Artist Makes a Living', *Picture Post*, 33, 12 (21 December 1946), 22-24, photographs by R. Kleboe.

1947   'The Job of a Rent Tribunal', *Picture Post*, 34, no. 3 (18 January 1947), 24-27, photographs by Haywood Magee.

1947   'Hypnotism: Science or Stunt?' *Picture Post*, 34, no. 2 (11 January 1947), 25-29, 31, photographs by Charles Hewitt.

1947   'Irish Storyteller', *Picture Post*, 34, no. 9 (15 March 1947), 21-25, photographs by Haywood Magee.

1947   'Trouble Among the Sugar-Cane', *Picture Post*, 34, no. 11 (29 March 1947), 21-23.

1947   'Britain's Heavyweight Hope', *Picture Post*, 35, no. 2 (12 April 1947), 19-20, photographs by Bert Hardy.

1947   'The "Haddocks" Make History', *Picture Post*, 35, no. 4 (26 April 1947), 10-13.

1947   'Christian Commandos Strike Again', *Picture Post*, 35, no. 5 (3

May 1947), 26-27, photographs by Bert Hardy.

1947	'Air Ambulance to the Isles', *Picture Post*, 35, no. 11 (14 June 1947), 18-21, photographs by Charles Hewitt.

1947	'Cowboys of the Carmargue', *Picture Post*, 36, no. 5 (2 August 1947), 8-11, photographs by Bert Hardy.

1947	'Mutiny in the Market Gardens', *Picture Post*, 36, no. 10 (6 September 1947), 19-21, photographs by Charles Hewitt.

1947	'Moravian Village', *Lilliput*, 21, no. 3 (September 1947), 242-48, photographs by Jan Lukas.

1947	'Germany's Child Smugglers', *Picture Post*, 37, no. 1 (4 October 1947), 7-11, photographs by Bert Hardy.

1947	'London's Health Ship', *Picture Post*, 37, no. 2 (11 October 1947), 27-29, photographs by Felix Mann.

1947	'Where the Acting's the Thing', *Picture Post*, 37, no. 7 (15 November 1947), 19-21, photographs by K. Hutton.

1947	'Do We Have Such Fun?', *Picture Post*, 37, no. 12 (20 December 1947), 22-25.

1948	'The Forgotten Gorbals', *Picture Post*, 38, no. 5 (31 January 1948), 11-16, photographs by Bert Hardy.

1948	'Eire Takes Hobson's Choice', *Picture Post*, 38, no. 8 (21 February 1948), 7-10, photographs by Bert Hardy.

1948	'Unicef Sets About the Job', *Picture Post*, 39, no. 4 (24 April 1948), 24-27.

1948	'The Night Watch on Crime', *Picture Post*, 39 no. 5 (1 May 1948), 19-21, photographs by Bill Brandt.

1948	'Henry Moore Prepares for Battersea', *Picture Post*, 39, no. 7 (15 May 1948), 25-27, photographs by Felix H. Mann.

1948	'Can We Save Our Iron Mines?', *Picture Post*, 39, no. 10 (5 June 1948), 7-9, photographs by Charles Hewitt.

1948	'Miss Dunham's Witchery', *Picture Post*, 39, no. 13, (26 June 1948), 11-13, photographs by Bert Hardy.

1948	'A Gypsy Family Invades London', *Picture Post*, 40, no. 1 (3 July 1948), 12-14, photographs by Felix H. Mann.

1948	'The Curious Art of the Palekh', *Lilliput*, 23, no. 4 (October 1948), 72-77.

1948	'Chelsea Gets a New Recruit', *Picture Post*, 41, no. 5 (30 October 1948), 10-13, photographs by Bert Hardy.

1948	'The Life of a Prison Officer', *Picture Post*, 41, no. 8 (20 November 1948), 8-15, photographs by Bert Hardy.

1948	'BOAC's Boss: The Fabulous Mr. Straight', *Picture Post*, 41, no. 10 (4 December 1948), 9-11, photographs by Bert Hardy.

1948	'A Village in France', *Picture Post*, 41, no. 12 (18 December 1948),

25-29, photographs by Bert Hardy.

1949 'Life in the Elephant', *Picture Post*, 42, no. 2 (8 January 1949), 10-16, photographs by Bert Hardy.

1949 'Slums Under the Trees', *Picture Post*, 42, no. 5 (29 January 1949), 7-11, photographs by Bert Hardy.

1949 'Splendours and Miseries of the Gaucho', *Lilliput*, 24, no. 2 (February 1949), 74-79; eight paintings by Molina Campos with commentary by A.L. Lloyd.

1949 'An Aboriginal Boy is Made a Man', *Picture Post*, 42, no. 7 (12 February 1949), 12-16.

1949 'The Boy Who Got On', *Picture Post*, 42, no. 11 (12 March 1949), 29-33.

1949 'Fishing in the Lofotens', *Picture Post*, 43, no. 5 (30 April 1949), 10-15, photographs by Haywood Magee.

1949 'Who'll Help the Refugee Arabs?', *Picture Post*, 43, no. 13 (25 June 1949), 12-17, photographs by Charles Hewitt.

1949 'Cowboy', *Picture Post*, 45, no. 2 (8 October 1949), 14-21, photographs by Leonard McCombe.

1949 'Rubbra: Heir of a Golden Age', *Picture Post*, 45, no. 11 (10 December 1949), 37-39, photographs by Haywood Magee.

1950 'A Shop-girl in Rio', *Picture Post*, 46, no. 5 (4 February 1950), 15-19.

1950 'Home of the Meat Ration', *Picture Post* (February/March? 1950).

1950 'A Visit to Buenos Aires', *Picture Post*, 46, no. 10 (11 March 1950), 14-19, 53, photographs by K. Hutton.

1950 'Down the Bay', *Picture Post* , 47, no. 4 (22 April 1950), 13-19, photographs by Bert Hardy.

1950 'Under the Gaucho Moon', *Lilliput*, 26, no. 6 (June 1950), 76-80; three paintings by Molina Campos with commentary by A.L. Lloyd.

1950 'Come All You Rounders', *Lilliput*, 27, no. 2 (August 1950), 101-104.

1950 'Down the Tyne', *Picture Post*, 49, no. 3 (21 October 1950), 13-19, photographs by Bert Hardy.

1950 'Penny for the Guy, Mister!' *Picture Post*, 49, no. 5 (4 November 1950), 31-33, photographs by Bert Hardy.

1950 'Wild and Woolly', *Lilliput*, 27, no. 5 (November 1950), 90-98, photographs by Lindsay Gutteridge.

1951 'St James' Infirmary', *Clubman* (April 1951).

1952 'Songs of Our Alley', *Lilliput*, 31, no. 4 (September/October 1952), 54-59.

1953 'London's Horse Market', *Lilliput*, 33, no. 5 (October/November 1953), 44-51, photographs by Thurston Hopkins.

1953	'Windows on a Dream World', *Lilliput*, 33, no. 6 (November/December 1953), 38, 116.

1954	'Folk-Song For Our Time', *The Marxist Quarterly*, no. 1 (January 1954), 47-56 (published by Lawrence and Wishart).

1954	'Folk Music Research'. A thesis for Degree of B. Arch., School of Architecture, King's College, Newcastle upon Tyne. By Kenneth Bell. Foreword by A.L. Lloyd (April 1954).

1954	'A Folk Song of the Industrial Revolution', *Sing*, 1, no. 2 (July/August 1954), 28-31 (notes and tune for 'The Poor Cotton Weaver').

1954	'The Singing Style of the Copper Family', *Journal of the English Folk Dance and Song Society*, 7 (1954), 145-51.

1955	'Old Jackie Brown' ('Go to Sea No More'), *Sing*, 1, no. 5 (January/February 1955), 106-107 (song and note).

1955	'Paddy West' *Sing*, 2, no. 1 (April/May 1955), 4 (song and note).

1955	'Some Notes on the "Which Side" Tune', *Sing*, 2, no. 2 (June/July 1955), 32.

1956	'Background to "St James' Infirmary"', *Sing*, 3, no. 2 (June/July 1956), 19-21 (revised from an article in *Keynote*, Workers' Music Association *c.* 1948).

1956	'The Bitter Withy', *Sing*, 3, no. 5 (December 1956/January 1957), 69 (song and note).

1957	'Johnny Todd', *Sing*, 3, no. 6 (February/March 1957), 79 (song and note).

1957	'Lord Franklin', *Sing*, 4, no. 3 (August/September 1957), 41 (song and note, collected by Lloyd in November 1937 from Edward Harper, a whale-factory blacksmith of Port Stanley in the Falklands).

1958	'Folk Instruments of Rumania, II, The Bucium', *British Rumanian Bulletin*, no. 1(?) (January 1958), 3.

1958	'Folk Instruments of Rumania, III, The Bagpipe', *British Rumanian Bulletin* (February 1958).

1958	'Folk Instruments of Rumania, IV, The Pan-pipes', *British Rumania Bulletin* (March 1958).

1958	'Folk Instruments of Rumania, V, The Cobza', *British Rumanian Bulletin* (April 1958).

1958	'So You Are Interested in Folk Music?', *Recorded Folk Music* (edited by A.L. Lloyd), no. 1 (January/February 1958), 1-9. Also 'Twenty Five Records for a Basic Collection', 6-9.

1958	'American Folk Song: The Present Situation', *Recorded Folk Music* (edited by A.L. Lloyd), 1, no. 2 (March/April 1958), 13-17; also 'Some Recommended Recordings of American Folk Music', 18-20.

1958   'Rumanian Folk Music: In Reality and on Disc', *Recorded Folk Music* (edited by A.L. Lloyd), 1, no. 3 (May/June 1958), 25-30.

1958   'Ethno-Musicology and Edmundo Ros', *Recorded Folk Music* (edited by A.L. Lloyd), 1, no. 4 (July/August 1958), 41-45; also 'Some Flamenco Recordings', 45-48.

1958   'Yugoslav Folk Music on Disc', *Recorded Folk Music* (edited by A.L. Lloyd), 1, no. 6 (November/December 1958), 61-65.

1958   'Notes to 5 Songs Collected by Peter Kennedy from Harry Cox', *Journal of the English Folk Dance and Song Society*, 8, no. 3 (December 1958); see also 'Miscegenation in Australian Folklore', *Journal of the English Folk Dance and Song Society*, 8, no. 4 (1959) for John Meredith's reply to A.L. Lloyd's notes, plus Lloyd's reply (p. 220).

1959   'The Street Singers of the French Revolution', *Recorded Folk Music* (edited by A.L. Lloyd), 2, no. 1 (January/February 1959), 6-10.

1959   'Folk Song as Urban Music', *Education*, 113, no. 2936 (May 1959), 932-35.

1959   'The Other Latin American Music', *Recorded Folk Music* (edited by A.L. Lloyd), 2, no. 3 (May/June 1959), 1-6.

1959   'How is Russian Folk Song Today?', *Recorded Folk Music* (edited by A.L. Lloyd), 2, no. 4 (July/August 1959), 1-6.

1959   'The Husband with No Courage in Him', *Sing Out* (Summer 1959), 10-11, song and note.

1959   'New Recordings of Bulgarian Folk Music', *Recorded Folk Music* (edited by A.L. Lloyd), 2, no. 5 (September/October 1959), 1-4.

1959   'The Lantari: New Light on the Gypsy Musician', *Recorded Folk Music* (edited by A.L. Lloyd), 2, no. 6 (November/December 1959), 6-9.

1959-60 'So You're Interested in Folk Music?', *Sing Out* (Winter 1959/60), 38-42; reprinted from *Recorded Folk Music* (no. 1, 1958).

—   *Songs from Bulgaria*, Workers' Music Association, Introduction by A.L. Lloyd, 195?.

1961   'The Folk-Song Revival', *Marxism Today* (June 1961), 170-73.

1961   'Folk Music in Eastern Europe Today', *Sing Out* (October/November 1961), 34-37; also letter on page 63 on song 'Poor Man's Heaven'.

—   'Folk Song and Modern Times', MSS (196?), 8pp.

1962   'Who Owns What in Folk Song?', *Sing Out* (February/March 1962), 41-43; also letter on page 61 on lack of protest songs in Eastern Europe.

1962   'The English Folk Song Revival', *Sing Out* (April/May 1962), 34–37.

1962   Leslie Shepard, *The Broadside Ballad*, Foreword by A.L. Lloyd, Herbert Jenkins, 205pp., 1962.

1963   'Rocking the Baby', *Sing*, 7, no. 7 (October 1963), 73, song and note.

1963   *Sing Out* (February/March 1963), 73; letter correcting spelling mistakes in previously published Russian song 'Koloda duda ide zh ty byla'.

1963   'Street Singers of the French Revolution', *Sing Out* (Summer 1963), 24–31; first published in *Recorded Folk Music* (January/February 1959); this version has new introduction plus music and lyrics for song 'Ca Ira'.

1963   'What's Traditional?', *Folk Music*, 1, no. 1 (November 1963), 10–13.

1963–64 'Music of the Rumanian Gypsies', *Proceedings of the Royal Musical Association*, 90th session (1963/64).

1964   'The Hullabaloo at Blaydon', *Sing Out* (April/May 1964), 34–37, with song 'Blaydon Races'.

1964   *Folk Scene* (October 1964); letter to editor saying that there is a need for magazine devoted to repertory rather than personalities.

1965   'Songs of the Dark Towns', *Albright Magazine* (April 1965).

1965   'The Tradition What Is It?', *Keele Festival Programme* (July 1965), 4–5.

1965   'Gypsy Music', *Recorded Sound* (Journal of the Institute of Recorded Sound), 19 (July 1965).

1965   'Sharp: Conclusion for 1965', *Folk Music*, 1, no. 10 (1965), 9–12.

1965   'The Bagpipe', *Romania Today* (August 1965).

1966   'How Outlandish is the Outlandish Knight?', *Tradition* (Folk-Song Society Magazine of the Students' Union, University College, London) 1, no. 1 (1966), 36–40.

1966   *Spin*, 5, no. 4 (1966); letter defending his own liking for amatory-encounter songs in reply to review in *Spin*, 5, no. 2, where he (Lloyd) was accused of 'boring over-emphasis on the sexual joke'.

1966   *Spin*, 'Guest Spot', 4, no. 4 (1966), 16–17. Article on innovation in the folk revival; reprinted from *Spin*, 1, no. 6.

1967   'Lady into Landscape: A Song and its History', *Chapbook*, 4, no. 5 (1967), 16–21. (Discusses: 'A Green leaf's a Green o', 'The Trooper's Horse', and 'North Sea Oil'. Words and music).

1967   'Further Notes on the James Duncan Collection', *Folk Music Journal*, 1 (1967), 181.

1967   'Songs of the Dark Towns', *Australian Tradition* (September 1967),

9-15, 31; originally in *Albright Magazine* (April 1965).

1968   'Albanian Folk Song', *Folk Music Journal*, 1 (1968), 202-22 and 15 musical examples.

1968   'How Folk Songs Get Around', *Sing*, 10, no. 2 (1968), 5-9; an extract from *Folk Song in England*, Lawrence and Wishart, 1967.

1969   'Walk Out St George?', *Spin*, 7, no. 1 (1969), 5-7, plus song.

1970   'The Overlander', *Club Folk* (January/February 1970), 15-16, song and note.

1970   'The Winds of the People' (poem), Miguel Hernandez, translated by A.L. Lloyd; *The Penguin Book of Socialist Verse*, edited by Alan Bold, Penguin Books, 550pp., 1970, p. 335; originally in *Poems for Spain*, Hogarth Press, 1939.

1970   'Lord Leitrim: A Little Known Irish Ballad', *Spin*, 7, no. 3 (1970).

1970   'Towards Distinction Between "Popular" and "Folk", a Bit of History', *Club Folk* (March/April 1970), 8-9.

1970   'Notes on Folklore and Folklore Collecting', *Tradition* (Magazine of the Folklore Society of Victoria and the Victorian Folk Music Club), no. 22 (May 1970), 3-5; originally published in the first Port Philip Festival Programme (date?).

1970   'Folklore and Australia', *Overland*, no. 45 (Autumn 1970), 17-26.

1971   'The Great European Wassail', *Spin*, 7, nos. 5 and 6 (1971), 4-8, plus 4 musical examples.

1973   'Folk-song Revivalists', *Observer Colour Magazine* (23 October 1973), 34, plus one page of colour photos of revival singers.

1973   *Real Sailor Songs*, John Ashton, Broadsheet King, November 1973, with an introduction by A.L. Lloyd.

1974   'The Donkey and the Zebra', *Folk Review*, 3, no. 11 (September 1974), 4-6; interview by Michael Grosvenor Myers with A.L. Lloyd.

1974-75 'Bartók and Folk Music: Documents, *Irish Folk Music Studies*, no. 2 (1974-75); a response to Hugh Shield's, 'Bartók and Folk Music' in *Irish Folk Music Studies*, no. 1.

1978   'On an Unpublished Irish Ballad' (Lord Leitrim), *Rebels and Their Causes*, essays in Honour of A.L. Morton, edited by Maurice Cornforth, Lawrence and Wishart, 224pp., 1978 (pp. 177-207).

1978   'The Ritual of the Calus: Any Light on the Morris?' *Folk Music Journal*, 3 (1978), 316-23.

1979   Review of *Songs of the Durham Coalfields* (Jock Purdon, Pit Lamp Press), *English Dance and Song*, 41, no. 1 (1979), 18.

1982   'Bouquet for Watersons', a tribute to the Watersons written for the Gold Badge Award Ceremony of the English Folk Dance and Song Society, MSS (August 1982).